X 8.00 EC/N

FRANK NORRIS: A BIBLIOGRAPHY

[Frank Norris from a photograph taken in spring, 1901.]

FRANK NORRIS

A Bibliography

COMPILED BY
Kenneth A. Lohf &
Eugene P. Sheehy

THE TALISMAN PRESS
Los Gatos, California 1959

Reprinted with the permission of the original publisher
KRAUS REPRINT CORPORATION
New York
1968

LIBRARY OF CONGRESS CATALOG NUMBER 59-14560

Printed in U.S.A.

CONTENTS

ILLUSTRATIONS

"No, it's not; no, it's not; no, it's not," cried Trina ve-
hemently. "It's all mine, mine. There's not a penny
of it belongs to anybody else. I don't like to have
to talk this way to you, but you just make me."
~~and besides when I~~ We're not going to touch a
penny of my five thousand nor a penny of that
little money I managed to save— that seventy-five."
"— That two hundred, ~~and fifty~~, you mean."
"— That seventy five. We're just going to live on the
interest of that and on what I earn from uncle
Oelberman— on just that thirty-one or two dollars."
"Huh! Think I'm going to do that, an' live in such
a room as this?"
Trina folded her arms and looked him squarely
in the face.
"Well, what are you going to do, then?"
"Huh?"
"I say, what are you going to do? You can get out
and find something to do and earn some more
money, and then we'll ~~talk~~ talk."
"Well, I ain't going to live here."
"Oh, very well, suit yourself. I'm going to live here."
"You'll live where I tell you," the dentist suddenly
cried, exasperated at the ~~[illegible]~~ humming tone she affected.
"Then you'll pay the rent," exclaimed Trina, quite
as angry as he.
"Are you my boss, I'd like to know? Who's the boss,
you or I?" cried Trina, flushing to her pale lips.
"Who's got the money, I'd like to know?" answer me
that, McTeague, who's got the money?"
"You make me sick, you and your money. Why,
you're a miser. I never saw anything like it. When
I was practising, I never thought of my fees as my
own; we lumped everything in together."
"Exactly; and I'm doing the working now. I'm
working for uncle Oelberman, and you're not

[Item 3]
Facsimile manuscript page of *McTeague* from the Argonaut Edition

PREFACE

The reader of Frank Norris' work is apt to be deceived by the order of publication of the individual novels, for the fiction was written in a different sequence from that in which it was published. The romances and stories of adventure were the author's first published works, although some of his important fiction was written at an earlier date.

Norris' development as a novelist falls into a number of clearly-defined stages. During his youth and years as an art student in Paris (1887-1889), he immersed himself in the medieval tradition of Froissart and the *Chanson de Roland,* and this interest culminated in the publication in 1892 of *Yvernelle,* a long narrative poem on a medieval theme. When, during his college years at the University of California and Harvard University (1890-1895), he came under the influence of Zola and, to a lesser extent, Kipling, his point of view matured and he produced some of his best writing, *McTeague* and *Vandover and the brute.* It was during his career as an editor for the San Francisco *Wave* and *McClure's Magazine* (1896-1899) that he wrote the romances, *Blix, Moran of the Lady Letty,* and *A man's woman,* which gained him acceptance in the literary world. Finally, during the last period (1899-1902) of his short life, when he was a reader for Doubleday and a free-lance writer, he began his trilogy, "The Epic of the Wheat," of which only the first two novels, *The octopus* and *The pit,* were completed.

McTeague was published in 1899, five years after Stephen Crane's *Maggie,* and these two novels were in large measure responsible for the break with the established genteel tradition and the rise of a new era of American realism notably advanced by Theodore Dreiser in *Sister*

Carrie. Most of Norris' work illustrates the impact of a new age and new attitude upon the forms and ideas of the nineteenth century; this is valid in the emotional as well as in the social areas.

Some critics will consider Norris a realist; others will maintain that he is a romanticist; and still others will call him a romantic realist. Actually, he was different things in varying degrees at different stages during his short but remarkably productive career. Robert Spiller in the *Literary history of the United States* has summed up the paradox: "He never achieved the discipline of the school to which he was instinctively allied, that of scientific naturalism, because his love of the story was too likely to run away with his ideas about it. Although he tried to reject the conventions and the sentimentality of popular romance, his critical distinctions were not sufficiently clear to keep him out of the traps against which he warned others."

A previous Norris bibliography by Joseph Gaer contained very abbreviated, and in some cases erroneous, data. Nevertheless, the Gaer work, together with the bibliographical information gleaned from Franklin D. Walker's biography of Norris, provided helpful guides for the compilation of what we have striven to make a complete and accurate record of Norris' published writings.

While we have concentrated on published works, a word about manuscript materials seems in order. A relatively small body of Norris manuscripts has survived, the largest collection being that in the Bancroft Library of the University of California. It includes the following noteworthy items: fifty letters, in holograph and photocopy, dated 1898-1902; a group of manuscript pages of *McTeague*; notes for *The octopus, The pit, and Vandover and the brute,* the manuscript map drawn for *The octopus*; manuscripts of the story, "Two hearts that beat as one," the article, "News gathering at Key West," and the poem, "Poitiers"; notes and drawings of medieval armor made at the Musée d'Artillerie in Paris; and various college themes, publishing contracts, and lists and manuscript reports made by Norris when he was a professional reader for Doubleday, Page and Company. In addition, there is a group of clippings of newspaper and periodical articles by and about Norris, as well as photocopies of manuscript items in other collections. The formation of this collection is the subject of a fascinating account by Dr. James D. Hart, Vice-Chancellor of the University of California (see item 376). The Bancroft Library is also the repository of a collection of research materials gathered by Dr. Franklin D. Walker in the preparation of his biography of Norris.

In the first section of this bibliography Norris' separately published works are entered chronologically by date of publication. Reprints of a given title follow in chronological order, with translations listed alphabetically by language. Owing to the very large number of periodical publications in the second major section of the bibliography, it seemed advisable to group these by genre, using an alphabetical title listing within each group. The final section is devoted to works about Norris, including a listing of contemporary reviews.

Many of the translations and a few of the reprint editions were not available to us, but these have been included only when complete information could be found in one of the national bibliographies. All other citations have been verified in the original sources. Of the many periodicals cited, the San Francisco *Wave* proved to be least accessible. The most complete file for the crucial period, 1896-1897, is held by the California State Library in Sacramento, and even their holdings lack the issues for July 11, 1896, August 28, 1897, and September 4, 1897. Partial files are held by the Bancroft Library (including the three missing issues previously noted), the Stanford University Library, the Sutro Branch of the California State Library, and the San Francisco Public Library.

For their help in verifying points of information, we are indebted to a great many friends and colleagues. Among those who have been particularly helpful are the following: George P. Hammond, John Barr Tompkins, Mrs. Elisabeth Gudde, and Miss Estelle Rebec of the Bancroft Library at the University of California; James D. Hart, University of California; Franklin D. Walker, Mills College; Paul L. Berry, Henry J. Dubester, and Frederick R. Goff, Library of Congress; Julius P. Barclay, Stanford University Library; Miss Christine L. Reb, University of Chicago Library; Robert Baumruk, Chicago Public Library; Mrs. Marian C. O'Donnell, San Francisco Public Library; and Bradford M. Hill, Boston Public Library. Lastly, we wish to acknowledge the assistance given us by Robert Greenwood and Newton Baird of the Talisman Press; it was they who first realized the need for a new, comprehensive bibliography and suggested that we undertake the work, and it was they who aided us in verifying the bulk of Norris' contributions to the *Wave*.

KENNETH A. LOHF
EUGENE P. SHEEHY

COLUMBIA UNIVERSITY LIBRARIES
NEW YORK CITY, SEPTEMBER 1959

PART I

WORKS BY FRANK NORRIS

Collected Works

1. ***THE COMPLETE WORKS OF FRANK NORRIS.*** *1898-1903*

   i. *The octopus.*

   The Complete Works of Frank Norris | THE OCTOPUS | The Epic of the Wheat | A STORY OF | CALIFORNIA | BY | Frank Norris | NEW YORK P. F. COLLIER & SON PUBLISHERS [title and author lines are enclosed within an engraving]

   473p. 21 x 14 ½ cm. Red cloth stamped in yellow on spine; volume number also stamped on spine. Frontispiece photograph of Norris by Arnold Genthe in volume one only.

   On verso of title-page: Copyright, 1901, by Doubleday, Page & Co.

   The remaining three volumes of the set are uniform with volume one:

   ii. *The pit; A deal in wheat.* c.1903. 432p.

   iii. *McTeague; A man's woman.* c.1899. 456p.

   iv. *Blix; Moran of the Lady Letty; Essays on authorship.* c.1898, 1899, and 1903. 382p. *Essays on authorship* is identical with *The responsibilities of the novelist.*

2. ***COMPLETE WORKS OF FRANK NORRIS.*** *1903*

   i. *Blix; Moran of the Lady Letty.*

   GOLDEN GATE EDITION | [panel line] | [ornament] | BLIX - MORAN | OF THE | LADY LETTY | COMPLETE | WORKS OF | FRANK | NORRIS | [ornament] | Published at New York by | Doubleday, Page & Co. | 1903 [title surrounded by double line border]

[viii] 341p. 25 x 16 cm. Blue paper over boards, tan cloth spine. Stamped in gold on cover, blue label on spine.

On page preceding half-title (p.[i]): This edition consists of one hundred sets, on Strathmore paper.

The remaining six volumes of the seven volume set are uniform with volume one:

ii. *A deal in wheat.* [x] 272p.
iii. *McTeague.* [vi] 442p.
iv. *A man's woman.* [viii] 286p.
v. *The octopus.* [x] 652p.
vi. *The pit.* [x] 421p.
vii. *The responsibilities of the novelist.* [vi] 311p.

3. ***THE ARGONAUT MANUSCRIPT LIMITED EDITION OF FRANK NORRIS'S WORKS.*** *1928*

i. *The octopus.*

THE OCTOPUS | A STORY OF CALIFORNIA | (I) | BY | FRANK NORRIS | WITH A FOREWORD BY | IRVIN S. COBB | VOLUME I | [publishers' device] | 1928 | DOUBLEDAY, DORAN & COMPANY, INC. | GARDEN CITY, NEW YORK

x, 274p. 23 x 15 cm. Simulated vellum over boards, with orange paper stripe near spine and orange paper corners; stamped in gold. Volume number and "The Argonaut Edition" stamped on spine. Photograph of Norris by Arnold Genthe appears as a frontispiece. Title of the set appears as a half-title.

On page preceding half title: This Argonaut Manuscript Edition is limited to two hundred and forty-five sets. . . .

Volume one of each set contains a page of the original *McTeague* manuscript.

The remaining nine volumes of the set are uniform with volume one:

ii. *The octopus* (II). 361p.

iii. (I) *Blix*; (II) *Moran of the Lady Letty.* xiii, 326p. Introductions by Kathleen Norris and Rupert Hughes.

iv. (I) *The third circle*; (II) *A deal in wheat.* ix, 332p. Introduction by Will Irwin.

v. *Vandover and the brute.* x, 311p. Foreword by Charles G. Norris. Introduction by H. L. Mencken.

vi. (I) *A man's woman*; (II) *Yvernelle.* x, 314p. Introduction by Christopher Morley.

vii. (I) *The responsibilities of the novelist*; (II) *The joyous miracle.* xli, 236p. Introduction by Caldwell Dobie. Forward by Grant Overton.

viii. *McTeague.* xi, 375p. Introduction by Theodore Dreiser.

ix. *The pit.* x, 403p. Introduction by Juliet Wilbor Tompkins.

x. *Collected writings hitherto unpublished in book form.* xiii, 335p. Introduction by Charles G. Norris.

Contents: Stories from the San Francisco *Wave*: The jongleur of Taillebois; A salvation boom in Matabeleland; The heroism of Jonesee; A case for Lombroso; His single blessedness; His dead mother's portrait; "Man proposes"—nos. 1-5.

Articles and sketches from the S .n Francisco *Wave*: Suggestions (I. 1870; II. A hotel bedroom; III. Brute); The end of the act; A South Sea expedition; New Year's at San Quentin; A "lag's" release; Among cliff dwellers; Sailing of the *Excelsior*; Passing of "Little Pete." Stories from the *Overland Monthly*: Lauth; Travis Hallett's half back; Outward and visible signs (I. She and the other fellow; II. The most noble conquest of man; III. Outside the Zenana; IV. After strange gods; V. Thoroughbred). South African articles: A Californian in the city of Cape Town; From Cape Town to Kimberley Mine; In the compound of a diamond mine; In the veldt of the Transvaal; A Zulu war dance; Jack Hammond in Johannesburg and Pretoria. Spanish War articles: With Lawton at El Caney; Santiago's surrender; *Comida*: an experience in famine. Later short stories: A statue in an old garden; A lost story; Buldy Jones, *chef de claque*.

4. *THE COMPLETE EDITION OF FRANK NORRIS. 1928*

Ten volumes. 22 x 15 cm. Black cloth stamped in gold on spine, with decoration depicting a sheaf of wheat. General title of edition from jacket.

Identical in content and format (except binding) with the "Argonaut Manuscript Limited Edition." Although the date, 1928, appears on the title-page, the set was not issued until early in 1929.

Individual Works

YVERNELLE. 1892

5. YVERNELLE | A LEGEND OF | FEUDAL FRANCE | BY | FRANK NORRIS | "Cui me moribundam deseris, hospes?" Aeneid | ILLUSTRATED | PHILADELPHIA | J B LIPPINCOTT Company | 1892 [title illuminated in colors]

116p. 23½ x 17 cm. Brown cloth stamped in gold on cover and spine. Some copies in full leather.

Illustrations by J. J. Bissegger, John J. Boyle, F. S. Church, C. M. Dewey, F. Dielman, E. H. Garrett, Charles L. Hinton, Will H. Low, E. Maene, and Walter Shirlaw.

Although the title-page bears the date, 1892, copies were released for sale late in 1891.

MORAN OF THE LADY LETTY. 1898

6. Moran of | The Lady Letty | [panel line] | A STORY OF ADVENTURE OFF | THE CALIFORNIA COAST :: :: | [panel line] | BY | FRANK NORRIS | [ornament with panel line above and below] | NEW YORK | DOUBLEDAY & McCLURE CO. | 1898 [title surrounded by a double line border]

[viii] 293p. 19 x 13 cm. Green cloth stamped in yellow and green on cover and spine. Some copies have top edges stained.

Dedication (p.[v]): Dedicated to Captain Joseph Hodgson, United States Life Saving Service.

Serialized in the San Francisco *Wave,* January 8-April 9, 1898; for complete information see item 59.

7. First English edition:

London, Grant Richards, 1899. 294p. (Under title *Shanghaied*)

8. Reprints:

Chicago, Jamieson-Higgins, 1902. (This edition is listed in the *United States Catalog Supplement, 1902-1905,* p. 1303; no copy located in American libraries)

New York, Doubleday, Page, 1904. 293p.

London, Grant Richards, 1904. 302p. (Under title *Shanghaied*)

Garden City, New York, Doubleday, Page, 1920. 293p.

London, T. Nelson, 1923. 290p. (Under title *Shanghaied*)

9. Translations:

Le matelot de le dame Loulou; roman d'aventures de la côte de Californie. Paris, L'Édition française illustrée [1921] viii, 247p. Tr., Albert Savine and Michel Georges-Michel.

L'Amazone de la mer. Paris, Michel, 1929. 83p. Tr., Jean Callot and Raoul Nicole.

Shanghaied. Leipzig, Linden-Verlag H. Fischer, 1937. 220p. Tr., Karl Sohm.

Der Ozean ruft. Linz, Pittsburgh, Wien, Ibis-Verlag, 1948 250p. Tr., Erich Gal.

Der Untergang der "Lady Letty." Linz, Demokrat Druck-u. Verl. Ges., 1952. 191p. Tr., Florence Palfrey.

Moran. Et Aeventyr fra Stillehavet. Copenhagen, Gyldendal, 1910. 200p. Tr., Aslaug Mikkelsen. 2nd ed.: 1920.

På eventyr i Stillehavet. Oslo, Napers [1945?] 185p. Tr., Arne Skjønhaug.

Moran Sternersen. Stockholm, Holmquist, 1914. 128p. Tr., Oscar Nachman.

Oceanens dotter. En aventyrsberättelse. Stockholm, Ahlén & Åkerlund, 1925. 258p. Tr., G. Sanden.

McTEAGUE. 1899

10. McTEAGUE | A Story of San Francisco | By FRANK NORRIS | AUTHOR OF "MORAN OF THE LADY LETTY" | [ornament with single panel line above and below] | NEW YORK | DOUBLEDAY & McCLURE CO. | 1899 [title enclosed in a single line border]

 [vi] 442p. 20½ x 13 cm. Red cloth stamped in yellow on cover and spine. First issue can be identified by the word "moment," which appears as the last word on p.106.

 Dedication (p.[v]) : Dedicated to L. E. Gates of Harvard University.

 A four-page article, "A New American Author," follows p.442. Of an advertising nature, it contains comment on *Moran of the Lady Letty* and a brief biographical sketch.

11. First English edition:

 London, Grant Richards, 1899. 442p.

12. Reprints:

 New York, Grosset & Dunlap [1899] 442p.

 New York, International Book & Publishing Co., 1900. 442p.

 New York, Grosset & Dunlap, 1907. 442p.

 New York, Boni and Liveright [1918] xiv, 442p. Introduction by Henry S. Pancost. (The Modern Library)

 Garden City, New York, Doubleday, Page, 1920. 442p.

 London, William Heinemann, 1922. 442p. New ed.

 Garden City, New York, Doubleday, Page, 1924. 442p. (Lambskin Library)

 New York, Grosset & Dunlap, 1925. 441p. With scenes from the photoplay.

MC TEAGUE
A Story of San Francisco
By FRANK NORRIS
AUTHOR OF "MORAN OF THE LADY LETTY"
NEW YORK
DOUBLEDAY & McCLURE CO.
1899

[Item 10]
Facsimile title-page from the first edition of *McTeague*

on opposite page

[Item 5]
Facsimile title page of *Yvernelle,* Frank Norris' first book.

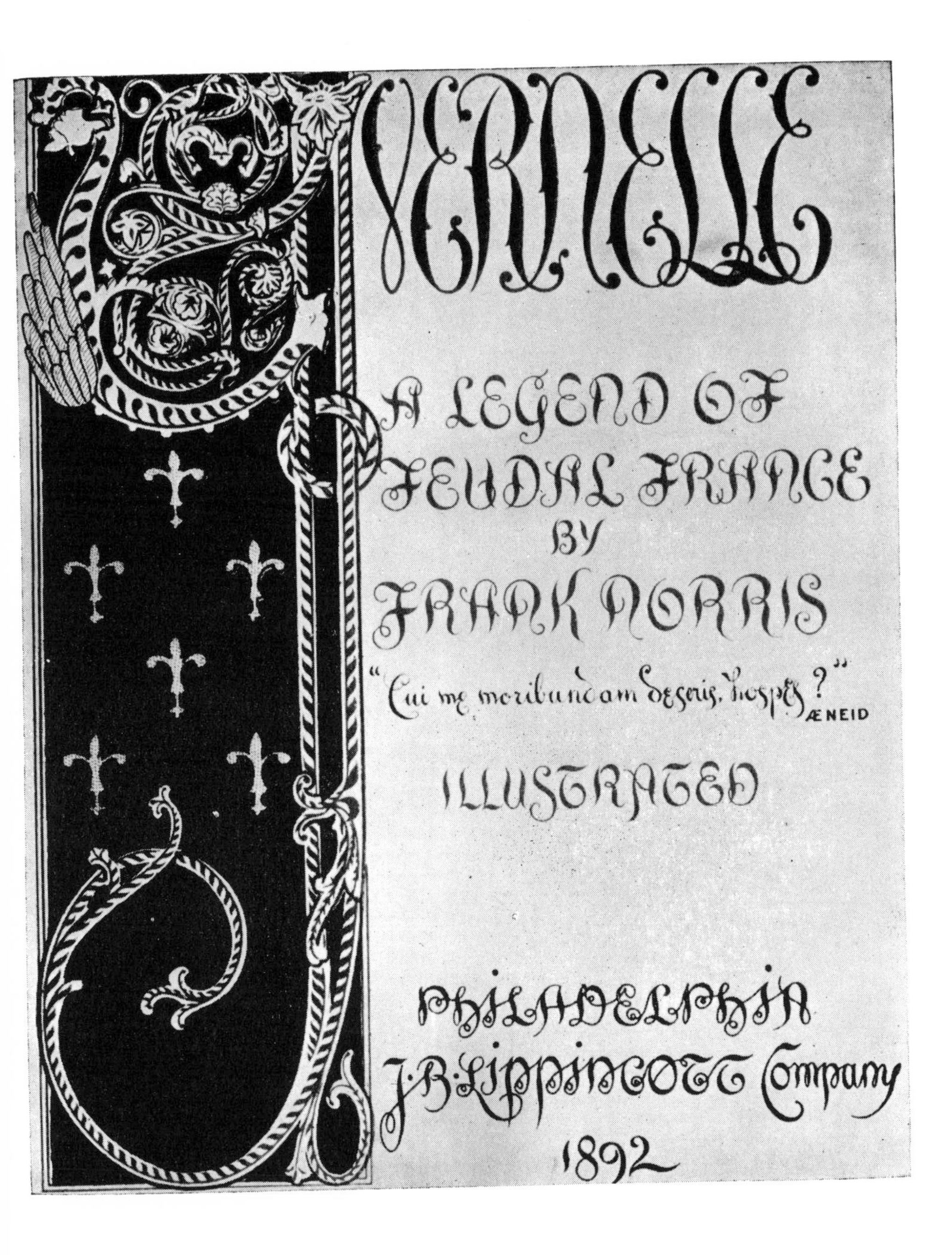

YVERNELLE

A LEGEND OF FEUDAL FRANCE

BY

FRANK NORRIS

"Cui me moribundam deseris, hospes?" ÆNEID

ILLUSTRATED

PHILADELPHIA

J·B·LIPPINCOTT Company

1892

San Francisco, Colt Press, 1941. 390p. Introduction by Charles G. Norris. Illustrations by Otis Oldfield. Note on title page: "An exact printing of the text from the first edition."

New York, Rinehart [1950] xix, 324p. Edited with an introduction by Carvel Collins. (Reinhart Editions, 40)

13. Translations:

McTeague. Copenhagen, Gyldendal, 1911. 348p. Tr., Aslaug Mikkelsen.

McTeague. Een verhaal uit San Francisco. Amsterdam, Ontwikkeling, 1926. 327p. Tr., A. Moresco.

Gier nach Gold. Leipzig, Linden-Verlag H. Fischer, 1937. 209p. Tr., Karl Sohm.

Verfluchtes Gold. Linz, Pittsburgh, Wien, Ibis-Verlag, 1947. 242p. Tr., Eberhart Frowein.

Shi no tani. Tokyo, Iwanami Shoten, 1957. 2 volumes. Tr., Eiji Ishida and Sôji Inoue.

BLIX. 1899

14. BLIX | by FRANK NORRIS | Author of McTeague | Moran of the | Lady Letty | etc. | [ornament] | New York | Doubleday & McClure Co. | 1899 [title enclosed in a double line border]

[vi] 339p. 19½ x 12½ cm. Tan cloth stamped in orange and black on cover and spine.

On verso of title-page (p.[iv]): Copyright, 1899, by Frank A. Munsey. Copyright, 1899, by Doubleday & McClure Co.

Dedication (p.[v]): Dedicated to my mother.

Serialized in the *Puritan,* March-August 1899; for complete information see item 57.

15. First English edition:

London, Grant Richards, 1900. 340p.

16. Reprints:

New York, Grosset & Dunlap [1899] 339p.

New York, International Association of Newspapers and Authors, 1901. 339p.

New York, Grosset & Dunlap, 1907. 339p.

Garden City, New York, Doubleday, Page, 1925. viii, 181p. Introduction by Kathleen Norris. (Lambskin Library, no.47)

17. Translations:

Blix. Copenhagen, Gyldendal, 1911. 196p. Tr., Vald. Rørdam. 2nd ed.: 1916.

Nuoruuden rakkautta. Helsinki, Jyväskylä, 1923. 208p. Tr., Irene Mendelin.

Bliks. Leningrad, Mysl, 1927. 196p. Tr., Y. I. Fortunato.

Ungdomskärlek. Stockholm, Nutiden, 1918. 152p.

Ungdomskärlek. Stockholm, Saxon & Lindström, 1933. 191p.

A MAN'S WOMAN. 1900

18. A MAN'S WOMAN | By FRANK NORRIS | [ornament with single panel line above and below] | New York | Doubleday & McClure Co. | 1900 [title enclosed in a single line border]

[vi] 286p. 20½ x 13 cm. Red cloth stamped in white. Green cloth binding stamped "Special Edition" at foot of spine is later issue. One page of publishers' advertisements at back.

Dedication (p.[v]): Dedicated to Dr. Albert J. Houston.

Author's note (p.[vi]): Reference is made to a play with the same title by Anne Crawford Flexner.

Serialized in the *San Francisco Chronicle,* July 23-October 8, 1899, and the *New York Evening Sun,*

September 25-October 17, 1899; for complete information see item 58.

19. First English edition:
    London, Grant Richards, 1900. 340p.

20. Reprints:
    New York, Doubleday, Page, 1904. 286p.
    New York, Doubleday, Page, 1905. 286p. (Crowned Masterpieces of Modern Fiction: Special Subscription Edition)
    New York, Grosset & Dunlap, 1907. 286p.
    Garden City, New York, Garden City Publishing Co., 1926. 286p. (Popular Copyrights)

21. Translations:
    En kvindes magt. Copenhagen, Gyldendal, 1912. 198p. Tr., Sten Drewsen. 2nd ed.: 1917.
    Naisen mahti. Helsinki, Jyväskylä, 1921. 252p. Tr., O. A. Joutsen.
    Silnaya dukhom. Leningrad, Mysl, 1928. 270p. Tr., Y. I. Fortunato.
    En kvinnas makt. Stockholm, Holmquist, 1917. 224p. Tr., A. Berg. 2nd ed.: 1926.

THE OCTOPUS. 1901

22. The Epic of the Wheat | THE OCTOPUS | A STORY OF CALIFORNIA | BY | FRANK NORRIS | [publishers' device] | NEW YORK | DOUBLEDAY, PAGE & CO. | 1901

    [viii] 652p. 20 x 13 cm. Red cloth stamped in gold on cover and spine. Many of the signature numbers lacking in later states; publisher's name on spine noted in two states.

    Dedication (p.[v]): Dedicated to my wife.

    For a discussion of the various printings of this novel see item 435.

Author's note on p.[viii] indicates that *The octopus* was to be the first novel of a projected trilogy dealing with "(1) the production, (2) the distribution, (3) the consumption of American wheat. When complete, they will form the story of a crop of wheat from the time of its sowing as seed in California to the time of its consumption as bread in a village of Western Europe." The second novel of the trilogy, *The pit,* was published in 1903; the last novel, to be entitled *The wolf,* was never written.

23. First English edition:
    London, Grant Richards, 1901. 656p.
24. Reprints:
    New York, Grosset & Dunlap, 1901. 652p.
    Leipzig, B. Tauchnitz, 1901. Two volumes. 335, 343p. (Collection of British Authors. Vol. 3542, 3543)
    New York, Doubleday, Page, 1903. 652p.
    Garden City, New York, Doubleday, Page, 1914. 652p.
    Garden City, New York, Doubleday, Page, 1920. 652p.
    London, T. Nelson, 1920. 576p. (Reprinted in 1923)
    New York, Doubleday, Page, 1922. 652p. (Lambskin Library)
    Garden City, New York, Doubleday, Doran, 1930. 361p.
    Garden City, New York, Sun Dial Press [1938] 274, 361p. (Hampton Court Edition)
    Garden City, New York, Doubleday, 1947. 361p.
    New York, Sagamore Press, 1957. 454p. Introduction by Robert D. Lundy. (American Century Series, S-20)

Boston, Houghton Mifflin, 1958. 448p. Introuction by Kenneth S. Lynn. (Riverside Editions)

New York, Bantam Books, 1958. 438p. (A Bantam Classic)

25. Translations:

Chobotnice. Prague, SNKLHU, 1957. 526p. Tr., Libuše Bubeníková and Jiři Valja.

Polypen. En Bog om Kalifornien. Copenhagen, Gyldendal, 1907. 384p. Tr., J. V. Jensen. 2nd ed.: 1918.

Le Pieuvre. Paris, Hachette, 1914. 264p. Tr., Arnelle.

Der Octopus. Stuttgart, Deutsche Verlags-Anstalt, 1907. 714p. Tr., Eugen von Tempsky.

Die goldene Fracht. Roman vom kalifornischen Weizen. Berlin, S. Fischer, 1940. 527p. Tr., Hermann Stresau.

Die goldene Fracht. Roman vom kalifornischen Weizen. Berlin, Deutsche Buch - Gemeinschaft, 1948. 549p. Tr., Hermann Stresau.

Die goldene Fracht. Linz, Pittsburgh, Wien, Ibis-Verlag, 1948. 244p. Tr., Fritz Benke.

Polypen. Oslo, Nationaltr., 1931. Two volumes. 242, 285p. Tr., Nils Lie.

Polyppen. Oslo, Gyldendal, 1951. 427p. Tr., Nils Lie.

Ośmiornica. Warsaw, Czytelnik, 1955. 534p. Tr., Tadeusz Dehnel and Wacława Komarnicka.

Sprut. Leningrad, Mysl, 1925. 351p. Tr., A. G. Edited by A. M. Karnaukhova.

Sprut. Simferopol, Proletari, 1925. 267p. Tr., P. Okhrimenko. Edited by M. Levidov.

Sprut. Moscow and Leningrad, Gosizdat, 1926. 111p. Tr. and abridged by E. K. Pimenova.

Polypen. Hvetets epos. En historia från Kalifornien. Stockholm, Ljus, 1908. Two volumes. 165, 224p.

Polip. Zagreb, "Zora," 1954. 504p. Tr., Šime Balen.

Polip. Ljubljana, Slovenski knjižni zavod., 1956. 390p. Tr., Bogo Pregelj.

THE PIT. 1903

26. The Epic of the Wheat | THE PIT | A STORY OF CHICAGO | BY | FRANK NORRIS | [publishers' device] | NEW YORK | DOUBLEDAY, PAGE & CO. | 1903

[viii] 421p. 21 x 14 cm. Special publishers' presentation edition, gray paper over boards with white label on spine. First trade edition is bound in red cloth stamped in gold. Frontispiece: Photograph of Norris.

On verso of title-page (p.[iv]): Copyright, 1902, by Curtis Publishing Co. Copyright, 1903, by Doubleday, Page & Co. Published February, 1903.

Dedication (p.[iv]): Dedicated to my brother Charles Gilman Norris.

Serialized in the *Saturday Evening Post,* September 20, 1902-January 31, 1903; for complete information see item 60.

27. First English edition:

London, Grant Richards, 1903. 430p.

28. Reprints:

[New York, c.1903] p.367-96. (Chapter X reprinted under the title: *The Panic Episode from F. Norris' . . . novel, "The pit," in William A. Brady's production . . . in which Wilton Lackaye appears as Curtis Jadwin*)

Garden City, New York, Garden City Publishing Co., 1903. 421p. (Lambskin Library)

New York, Grosset & Dunlap, 1903. 421p.
Leipzig, B. Tauchnitz, 1905. Two volumes. 264, 296p. (Collection of British Authors. Vols. 3654, 3655)
New York, A. Wessels, 1906. 421p.
Garden City, New York, Doubleday, Page, 1920. 421p.
London, T. Nelson, 1920. 384p. (Reprinted in 1924 and 1935)
New York, Doubleday, Page, 1922. 421p. (Lambskin Library)
New York, Grosset & Dunlap [192-?] 421p.
Garden City, New York, Doubleday, Doran, 1930. 403p.
New York, The Modern Library [1934] x, 403p.
New York, T. Nelson, 1935. 384p.
Garden City, New York, Sun Dial Press [1937] 403p. (Hampton Court Edition)
New York, Grove Press [1956] 421p. (An Evergreen Book, E-41)
London, John Calder, 1956. viii, 421p.

29. Translations:
Malstrommen. En Bog om Chicago. Copenhagen, Gyldendal, 1909. 278p. Tr., Sten Drewsen.
Syvänne. Helsinki, Viipuri, 1914. 201p. Tr., Yrjö Sirola.
Die Getreidebörse. Stuttgart, Deutsche Verlags-Anstalt, 1912. 427p. Tr., Eugen von Tempsky.
Kampf um Millionen. Ein Roman aus Chikago. Berlin, Schildhorn-Verlag, 1935. 228p. Tr., Karl Sohm.
Az örvény. Budapest, Tolnai, 1936. 317p. Tr., Zoltán Bartos.
Malstrømmen. Oslo, Reistad, 1940. 294p. Tr., Nils Lie.

Omut. Leningrad, Mysl, 1925. 373p. Tr., A. G.
Hvirfveln. En historia om Chicago. Stockholm, Fahlcrantz, 1904. Two volumes. 198, 172p. Tr., H. Flygare.

THE RESPONSIBILITIES OF THE NOVELIST. *1903*

30. THE RESPONSIBILITIES | OF THE NOVELIST | AND OTHER LITERARY | ESSAYS | BY | FRANK NORRIS | [vignette] | NEW YORK | DOUBLEDAY, PAGE & COMPANY | 1903

[vi] 311p. 20 x 14 cm. Green cloth stamped in gold on cover and spine. First state has untrimmed edges.

On verso of title-page (p.[iv]): Copyright, 1902, by the Critic Publishing Company. Copyright, 1901, 1902, 1903, by Doubleday, Page & Company. Published, September, 1903.

Contents: The responsibilities of the novelist; The true reward of the novelist; The novel with a "purpose"; Story-tellers vs. novelists; The need of a literary conscience; A neglected epic; The frontier gone at last; The great American novelist; New York as a literary centre; The American public and "popular" fiction; Child stories for adults; Newspaper criticisms and American fiction; Novelists to order—while you wait; The "nature" revival in literature; The mechanics of fiction; Fiction writing as a business; The "volunteer manuscript"; Retail bookseller: literary dictator; An American school of fiction?; Novelists of the future; A plea for romantic fiction; A problem in fiction; Why women should write the best novels; Simplicity in art; Salt and sincerity; Bibliography, essays, articles, letters; Short stories; Poems published; Books published.

31. First English edition:
London, Grant Richards, 1903. 316p.
32. Reprint:
New York, Alicat Bookshop Press, 1949. 35p. (The Outcast Chapbooks, 15) A selection entitled: *Six essays on the responsibilities of the novelist.*
Contents: The responsibilities of the novelist; The true reward of the novelist; The novel with a "purpose"; The need of a literary conscience; Simplicity in art; Novelists of the future.

A DEAL IN WHEAT. 1903

33. A DEAL IN WHEAT | AND OTHER STORIES OF | THE NEW AND OLD WEST | BY | FRANK NORRIS | Illustrated by Remington, Leyendecker, Hitchcock and Hooper | [ornament] | NEW YORK | DOUBLEDAY, PAGE & COMPANY | 1903
[viii] 272p. 21 x 14 cm. Red cloth stamped in gold on cover and spine. Various shades of red cloth binding noted.
Contents: A deal in wheat; The wife of Chino; A bargain with Peg-Leg; The passing of Cock-Eye Blacklock; A memorandum of sudden death; Two hearts that beat as one; The dual personality of Slick Dick Nickerson; The ship that saw a ghost; The ghost in the crosstrees; The riding of Felipe.
34. First English edition:
London, Grant Richards, 1903. 280p.
35. Reprints:
New York, Grosset & Dunlap, 1903. 272p.
New York, A. Wessels, 1907. 272p.
36. Translations:
Komugi sôba; Takibi. Tokyo, Eihô-Sha, 1956. 188p.
Tr., Kyôichi Ono and Motoo Takigawa.

Sdelka s pshenitsei. In: *Amerikanskaya novella XIX veka.* Edited and with an introduction by A. Startsev. Moscow, Goslitizdat, 1946.

THE JOYOUS MIRACLE. 1906

37. THE | JOYOUS MIRACLE | [panel lines] | BY | FRANK NORRIS | [publishers' device] | NEW YORK | DOUBLEDAY, PAGE & COMPANY | MCMVI [double row of panel lines at end of imprint; title enclosed in ornamental border]

[vi] 27p. 19½ x 13 cm. Yellow paper over boards, white paper spine, stamped in gold on cover.

On verso of title-page (p.[iv]): Copyright, 1898, by the S. S. McClure Company. Copyright, 1906, by Doubleday, Page & Company. Published, October, 1906. Designed and printed by the University Press, Cambridge, U. S. A.

38. First English edition:

London, Harper & Brothers, 1906. 32p.

39. Reprint:

Garden City, New York, Doubleday, Doran, 1941. 21p. (With cover sub-title: *A parable of Christmas*)

THE THIRD CIRCLE. 1909

40. THE THIRD CIRCLE | BY | FRANK NORRIS | AUTHOR OF "THE PIT," "THE OCTOPUS," ETC. | INTRODUCTION BY | WILL IRWIN | NEW YORK: JOHN LANE COMPANY | LONDON : JOHN LANE, THE BODLEY HEAD | MCMIX

298p. 19½ x 13 cm. Red cloth stamped in gold on cover and spine. Four pages of publishers' advertisements at the back. Frontispiece: Photograph of Frank Norris.

Introduction by Will Irwin appears on p.7-11 and is dated March 1909.

Contents: The third circle; The house with the blinds; Little dramas of the curbstone; Shorty Stack, pugilist; The strangest thing; A reversion to type; "Boom"; The dis-associated charities; Son of a sheik; A defense of the flag; Toppan; A caged lion; "This animal of a Buldy Jones"; Dying fires; Grettir at Drangey; The guest of honor.

41. First English edition:
London, John Lane, 1909. 298p. Introduction by Will Irwin.

42. Reprints:
New York and London, John Lane, 1914. 298p. New ed. Introduction by Will Irwin. (Reprinted in 1923)

43. Translation:
Toppan. Leningrad, Seyatel, 1926. 45p. Tr., M. Matveyeva. (A translation of one of the stories from *The third circle*)

VANDOVER AND THE BRUTE. 1914

44. VANDOVER AND THE | BRUTE | [double ruled lines] | BY | FRANK NORRIS | [publishers' device] | [double ruled lines] | DOUBLEDAY, PAGE & COMPANY | GARDEN CITY NEW YORK | 1914

ix, 354p. 19½ x 13 cm. Boards, paper label; also advance issue, cloth back. First trade edition, red cloth stamped in gold on spine and cover.

Colophon: The Country Life Press, Garden City, New York.

A Foreword by Charles G. Norris appears on p.v-ix and is dated February, 1914.

45. First English edition:
    London, William Heinemann, 1914. 320p.
46. Reprints:
    New York, Grove Press, 1959. 354p. (An Evergreen Book, E-148)
    London, John Calder, 1959. 354p.
47. Translation:
    Dyret. Copenhagen, John Martin, 1915. 272p. Tr., Jesper Ewald.

THE SURRENDER OF SANTIAGO. 1917

48. THE SURRENDER | OF SANTIAGO | AN ACCOUNT OF THE | HISTORIC SURRENDER OF SANITAGO | TO GENERAL SHAFTER | JULY 17, 1898 | BY FRANK NORRIS | [ornament] | SAN FRANCISCO | PAUL ELDER AND COMPANY | NINETEEN SEVENTEEN

    24p. 16½ x 13 cm. Tan paper wrappers stamped in black, with drawing in black and orange.

    On verso of title-page (p.[2]): Copyright, 1913, 1917 by Otis F. Wood.

    Colophon: Published for the benefit of the Red Cross Funds. . . . first published by Otis F. Wood, in the Sun, New York. . . . Issued by Paul Elder & Company at their Tomoye Press, under the direction of Ricardo J. Orozco, in May, nineteen seventeen.

    For the appearance in the *New York Sun* see item 261.

TWO POEMS AND "KIM" REVIEWED. 1930

49. FRANK NORRIS: | TWO POEMS AND | "KIM" REVIEWED. | with a BIBLIOGRAPHY | by HARVEY TAYLOR. | [ornament] | HARVEY TALOR | SAN FRANCISCO | 1930

Unpaged ([44]p.) 21 x 14 cm. Blue paper over boards, white cloth spine, label on cover. Wood-cut portrait of Norris by Clairice Collins appears as frontispiece. An original Charles G. Norris letter was inserted in the first 25 copies.

Colophon: . . . two hundred copies have been printed by the Calmar Press. . . . . Each copy is numbered, and signed by the publisher, and the artist.

Contents: Crepusculum; Brunhilde; Mr. Kipling's "Kim"; The first editions of Frank Norris. A bibliography; Bibliographical index.

The prose piece, *A review of Kim* ([Sacramento, California, 1934] [7]p.), was separately published in an edition of 275 copies.

FRANK NORRIS OF "THE WAVE." 1931

50. FRANK NORRIS | OF "THE WAVE" [vignette] Stories | & Sketches from the San Francisco | weekly, 1893 to 1897. [vignette] Foreword | by Charles G. Norris. Introduction by | Oscar Lewis | [line-drawing] | 1931 | San Francisco :: The Westgate Press | [double line]

[xii] 250p. 24 x 16½ cm. Decorated yellow paper over boards; brown cloth spine with label.

On verso of title-page (p.[ii]): Copyright 1931, by The Westgate Press.

Colophon: 500 copies printed by The Grabhorn Press in February 1931.

The Foreword by Charles G. Norris appears on p.[v-vii], and the Introduction by Oscar Lewis on p.1-15.

Contents: Bandy Callaghan's girl; His sister; End of the beginning; Judy's service of gold plate; Fantaisie printaniere; Perveted tales; The Santa Cruz

Venetian carnival; A California jubilee; Hunting human game; The bombardment; At home from eight to twelve; Cosmopolitan San Francisco; Reviews and interviews; In the heat of battle; The puppets and the puppy; Through a glass darkly; The Isabella Regina; A miner interviewed; When a woman hesitates; Western city types; The opinions of Leander.

The volume also contains pen-and-ink sketches reprinted from the *Blue and Gold: The University of California Annual, Class of 1893* and *Class of 1894.*

Distributed in England by Simpkin Marshall.

THE LETTERS. 1956

51. THE • LETTERS • OF | FRANK | NORRIS | [ornament] | EDITED BY FRANKLIN WALKER | SAN FRANCISCO | The Book Club of California | MCMLVI

xiii, 99p. 29 x 21 cm. Red cloth spine, decorated boards, label on spine. Frontispiece: Portrait of Norris owned by Dr. Frank Norris and on deposit in the Bancroft Library.

Colophon: Three hundred and fifty copies printed by Edwin & Robert Grabhorn for the Colt Press.

The Introduction by Franklin Walker appears on p.v-xi

A number of letters were reprinted from previously published works: six letters from Isaac F. Marcosson's *Adventures in interviewing*; one letter from Mildred Howells' *Life and letters of W. D. Howells*; three letters (to Ernest Peixotto) from the *Saturday Review,* May 27, 1933; one letter from Nellie Sanchez' *The life of Mrs. Robert Louis Stevenson.*

Also included in the volume is an essay, "News gathering at Key West," written by Norris during the Spanish-American War.

Dramatizations

52. *The pit.* Play in four acts adapted by Channing Pollock from the Frank Norris novel. Produced by William A. Brady at the Lyric Theatre, New York, February 10, 1904. 77 performances.

    For a listing of the cast see: *The best plays of 1899-1909.* Edited by Burns Mantle and Garrison P. Sherwood. Philadelphia, Blakiston, 1944. p.454.

    Reviews: *New York Tribune* February 11, 1904, p.11a (William Winter); *Theatre; an illustrated magazine of theatrical and musical life* (New York) 4:57-58 March 1904.

    A typescript of the play is on file in the Harvard University Library.

53. *The guest of honour.* A play in one act by Christopher Marie St. John. "Founded on a story by . . . Frank Norris." [London? 19—]

    A typescript, 29p., is on file in the Theatre Collection of the New York Public Library.

Film Adaptations

54. *McTeague*. (Under title "Greed") Metro-Goldwyn, 1924. Written and directed by Erich von Stroheim. Edited by June Mathis. Photography by Ben Reynolds, William Daniels, and Ernest Schoedsack. Cast: Gibson Gowland, Jean Hersholt, Zasu Pitts, Chester Conklin, and Dale Fuller.

    For a listing of reviews and discussions of the film see: *The Film Index,* volume 1 (New York, 1941), p.407-08.

    An earlier film version, entitled "Life's Whirlpool," was produced in 1915 by the World Film Corporation, and starred Fania Marinoff and Holbrook Blinn.

55. *Moran of the Lady Letty*. c. Famous Players-Lasky Corp., 1922. Director, George Melford; adaptation, Monte M. Katterjohn. Cast: Rudolph Valentino and Doris Dalton.

56. *The pit*. William A. Brady's Picture Plays, Inc., 1917. c. World Film Corporation. Adaptation, Maurice Tourneur.

Contributions to Periodicals

Serializations

57. *Blix. Puritan* (New York) 5:229-41, 394-408, 635-48; 6:74-88, 254-64, 427-40 March-August 1899.
58. *A man's woman. San Francisco Chronicle* July 23-October 8, 1899; *New York Evening Sun* September 25-October 17, 1899. Appeared daily.
59. *Moran of the Lady Letty. Wave* 17,no.2:9; no.3:5; no.4:6-7; no.5:5-6; no.6:6-7; no.7:5; no.8:5-6; no.-9:5-6; no.11:5-6; no.12:5; no.13:5-6; no.14:5-6; no.-15:5-6. January 8-April 9, 1898.
60. *The pit. Saturday Evening Post* vol. 175, September 20, p.1-3, 18-19; September 27, p.10-11, 19; October 4, 10-11; October 11, p.9-11, 24; October 18, p.9-11, 18-19; October 25, p.10-12, 30-32; November 1, p.13-14, 18-19; November 8, p.6-7, 24; November 15, p.9-11, 20; November 22, p.10-11; November 29, p.9-11, 20; December 6, p.14-15,38; December 13, p.10-11, 20; December 20, p.10-11, 20; December 27, p.10-11, 18-19; January 3, p.10-11, 20; January 10, p.10-11; January 17, p.10-11, 18-19; January 24, p.10-11, 20; January 31, p.13-15. 1902-03.

Poetry

61. At Damietta, A.D. 1250. *Occident* 19:74-75 October 31, 1890. (Signed "Norrys")
62. Brunehilde. *Occident* 19:110 November 21, 1890 (Signed "Norrys") Reprinted: *Californian Illustrated Magazine* 2:61-63 June 1892. Illustrated by Norris. (In all reprintings title is spelled "Brunhilde").
63. Crepusculum. *Overland Monthly* s.2,19:347 April 1892.

Reprinted: Mighels, Ella S. C. *The story of the files.* [San Francisco] c.1893. p.360.

64. Les enervés de Jumiéges. *Occident* 19:135 December 12, 1890. (Signed "Norrys")
65. The exile's toast. *Reader* 9:684 May 1907.
66. Poitiers. This poem was listed in the Gaer bibliography and in *The responsibilities of the novelist* as having been published in the *Berkeleyan Magazine* in 1891. A search of that periodical, and other publications of the University of California for the period, failed to turn up an appearance of the poem. There is, however, a manuscript copy in the Norris Collection of the Bancroft Library.

Short Stories

(Including dramatic pieces)

67. Arachne. *Wave* 9,no.3:3 July 26, 1892.
68. At home from eight to twelve. *Wave* 17,no.1:7 January 1, 1898.
69. Bandy Callaghan's girl. *Wave* 15,no.16:4-5 April 18, 1896.
70. A bargain with Peg-leg. *Collier's Weekly* 28:13,16 March 1, 1902.
71. "Boom." *Wave* 16,no.32:5 August 7, 1897.
72. Buldy Jones, *chef de claque. Everybody's Magazine* 4:449-59 May 1901.
73. A caged lion. *Argonaut* August 20, 1894, p.4. Reprinted: *Argonaut* 51:328 November 17, 1902; *Argonaut stories.* San Francisco, Payot, Upham, 1906. p.13-23.
74. A case for Lombroso. *Wave* 16,no.37:6 September 11, 1897.
75. A deal in wheat. *Everybody's Magazine* 7:173-80 August 1902. Illustrated by J. C. Leyendecker. Re-

printed: *To-day; A Weekly Magazine Journal* (London) 38:385-88 April 22, 1903.

76. A defense of the flag. *Argonaut* October 28, 1895, p.4.
77. The drowned who do not die. *Wave* 18,no.13:9,12 September 24, 1898.
78. The dual personality of Slick Dick Nickerson. *Collier's Weekly* 30:8-9,22-23 November 22, 1902.
79. Dying fires. *Smart Set* 7,no.3:95-101 July 1902.
80. The end of the act. *Harvard Advocate* 59,no.1:13-14 April 3, 1895. Reprinted: *Wave* 16,no.48:3 November 27, 1897.
81. The end of the beginning. *Wave* 16,no.36:5 September 4, 1897.
82. Execution without judgment. *Wave* 16,no.40:5 October 2, 1897.
83. Fantaisie printaniere. *Wave* 16,no.45:7 November 6, 1897.
84. The finding of Lieutenant Outhwaite. *Occident* 20, no.5:49-51 March 13, 1891. (Signed "Norrys")
85. The ghost in the cross-trees. *New York Herald Literary Section* March 1, 1903, p.3.
86. The great Szarratar opal. *Smiles* (University of California) 1,no.3:6 November 18, 1891.
87. Grettir at Drangey. *Everybody's Magazine* 6:257-65 March 1902.
88. Grettir at Thornhall-Stead. *Everybody's Magazine* 8:311-19 April 1903.
89. The guest of honor. *Pilgrim* (Battle Creek, Michigan) 6:8,22 July 1902; 6:9,32-33 August 1902.
90. The heroism of Jonesee. *Wave* 15,no.20:6 May 16, 1896.
91. His dead mother's portrait. *Wave* 16,no.46:8-9 November 13, 1897.

92. His single blessedness. *Wave* 16,no.38:6 September 18, 1897.
93. His sister. *Wave* 15,no.48:7 November 28, 1896.
94. The house with the blinds. *Wave* 16,no.34:5 August 21, 1897.
95. In the heat of battle. *Wave* 15,no.51:6-7 December 19, 1896. (A short play)
96. The Isabella Regina. *Wave* 16,no.48:6 November 27, 1897. (A dialogue)
97. Le jongleur de Taillebois. *Wave* 7,no.33:6-9 December 25, 1891.
98. Judy's service of gold plate. *Wave* 16,no.42:6 October 16, 1897.
99. Kirkland at quarter. *Saturday Evening Post* 174:4-5 October 12, 1901.
100. Lauth. *Overland Monthly* s.2,21:241-60 March 1893. Illustrated with pen-and-ink drawings by Norris.
101. Little dramas of the curbstone. *Wave* 16,no.26:9 June 26, 1897.
102. A lost story. *Century Magazine* 66(n.s.44):371-79 July 1903. Illustrated by Christine S. Bredin. Reprinted: *The Spinners' book of fiction.* San Francisco, Paul Elder [1907] p.221-42.
103. "Man proposes"—No. 1. *Wave* 15,no.21:6 May 23, 1896.
104. "Man proposes"—No. 2. *Wave* 15,no.22:7 May 30, 1896.
105. "Man proposes"—No. 3. *Wave* 15,no.24:9 June 13, 1896.
106. "Man proposes"—No. 4. *Wave* 15,no.26:9 June 27, 1896.
107. "Man proposes"—No. 5. *Wave* 15,no.27:12 July 4, 1896.

108. A memorandum of sudden death. *Collier's Weekly* 28:11,14-15 January 11, 1902.
109. Miracle joyeux. *Wave* 16,no.41:4 October 9, 1897. Reprinted: *McClure's Magazine* 12:154-60 December 1898.
110. Outward and visible signs. Illustrated with pen-and-ink drawings by Norris. A series of five stories as follows:
    I. She and the other fellow. *Overland Monthly* s.2,23:241-46 March 1894; II. The most noble conquest of man. *Overland Monthly* s.2,23: 502-06 May 1894; III. Outside the zenana. *Overland Monthly* s.2,24:82-86 July 1894; IV. After strange gods. *Overland Monthly* s.2,24:375-79 October 1894; V. Thoroughbred. *Overland Monthly* s.2,25:196-201 February 1895.
111. The passing of Cock-eye Blacklock. *Century Magazine* 64(n.s.42):385-91 July 1902. Illustrated by J. N. Marchand. Reprinted: *The California story book.* [Berkeley, 1909] p.[1-19]
112. The puppets and the puppy. *Wave* 16,no.21:5 May 22, 1897. (A dialogue)
113. Reversion to type. *Wave* 16,no.33:5 August 14, 1897.
114. The riding of Felipe. *Everybody's Magazine* 4:254-66 March 1901.
115. A salvation boom in Matabeleland. *Wave* 15,no.17:5 April 25, 1896.
116. The ship that saw a ghost. *Overland Monthly* s.2,40:489-99 December 1902; *New England Magazine* n.s. 27:439-49 December 1902.
117. Shorty Stack, pugilist. *Wave* 16,no.47:5-6 November 20, 1897.

118. The son of a sheik. *Argonaut* June 1, 1891, p.6. (Unsigned) Norris' original title for this story was "Babazzouin."
119. A statue in an old garden. *Ladies' Home Journal* 20:4 May 1903.
120. The story of the seven sports, or the genie of the barrel. *Blue and gold: the University of California annual, class of 1894.* San Francisco, 1893. p.218-22. Illustrated with pen-and-ink sketches by Norris. Unsigned, but attributed to Norris by Harvey Taylor.
121. The strangest thing. *Wave* 16,no.27:7 July 3, 1897.
122. A thief for twenty minutes. *Wave* 16,no.23:5 June 5, 1897. (Signed "Justin Sturgis")
123. The third circle. *Wave* 16,no.35:5 August 28, 1897.
124. This animal of a Buldy Jones. *Wave* 16,no.29:5 July 17, 1897. Reprinted: *McClure's Magazine* 12:438-41 March 1899.
125. Through a glass darkly. *Wave* 16,no.24:5 June 12, 1897. (A dialogue)
126. Travis Hallett's half-back. *Overland Monthly* s.2,23:20-27 January 1894. Illustrated with pen-and-ink sketches by Norris. Reprinted: *Under the Berkeley oaks.* San Francisco, A. M. Robertson, 1901. p.9-36.
127. Two hearts that beat as one. *Ainslee's* 10:52-58 January 1903; *Idler* (London) 22:623-27 February 1903.
128. Two pair. A farce in one act. Presented by the Junior class, December 10, 1892. Scenes IV-VII. *Blue and gold: the University of California annual, class of 1894.* San Francisco, 1893. p.183-92. Illustrated with pen-and-ink sketches by Norris.

Reprinted: *California play and pageant.* [Berkeley, 1913] Unpaged.

129. Unequally yoked. *Berkeleyan Magazine* 2:44-48 September 22, 1893. Reprinted as "Toppan" in *The third circle.*

130. The way of the world. *Wave* 9,no.3:3-4 July 26, 1892.

131. The wife of Chino. *Century Magazine* 65(n.s.43): 369-78 January 1903. Illustrated by J. N. Marchand.

Articles & Sketches

132. American diplomats. *Wave* 17,no.3:6-7 January 15, 1898. (Signed "Justin Sturgis")
133. The American public and popular fiction. Syndicated February 2, 1903. Newspaper appearance not verified.
134. An American school of fiction? A denial. *Boston Evening Transcript* January 22, 1902, p.17.
135. Among the cliff dwellers. *Wave* 16,no.20:6 May 15, 1897.
136. Art Association exhibit. *Wave* 16,no.48:6 November 27, 1897. (Signed "Justin Sturgis")
137. The associated un-charities. *Wave* 16,no.44:7 October 30, 1897.
138. Belasco on plays. *Wave* 16,no.35:10 August 28, 1897. An interview with David Belasco.
139. The benefit field day for the California-Eastern team. *Wave* 15,no.19:6 May 9, 1896. (Unsigned)
140. A bicycle Gymkhana. *Wave* 16,no.28:9 July 10, 1897. (Signed "Justin Sturgis")
141. A bitter bit. *Wave* 16,no.16:6 April 17, 1897. (Signed "Justin Sturgis")
142. The Bivalve at home. *Wave* 15,no.40:5 October 3, 1896.
143. The bombardment. *Wave* 16,no.14:5 April 3, 1897. (Signed "Justin Sturgis")
144. Books and writers of current interest discussed especially for the Chicago American's literary review by the author of "The octopus," "McTeague," "Moran of the Lady Letty," etc. *Chicago American Literary Review* May 25, p.8; June 1, p.5; June 8, p.5; June 15, p.5; June 22, p.8; June 29, p.8; July 6, p.8; July 13, p.8; July 20, p.8; August 3, p.5; August 10, p.8; August 24, p.8; August 31,

p.8. 1901. (May 25 is a "Special Letter" entitled "Literature in the East")

145. A California artist. *Wave* 16,no.6:9 February 6, 1897.
146. A California jubilee. *Wave* 15,no.28:7 July 11, 1896.
147. A California vintage. *Wave* 14,no.41:7 October 12, 1895.
148. A Californian in the city of Cape Town. Characteristics of its mixed population of English, Dutch, Malays, French and Kaffirs. *San Francisco Chronicle* January 19, 1896, p.19.
149. A cat and dog life. *Wave* 16,no.32:6 August 7, 1897.
150. Chances of unknown writers. Syndicated March 2, 1903. Newspaper appearance not verified.
151. Child stories for adults. Syndicated February 9, 1903. Newspaper appearance not verified.
152. The class of '94. *Blue and gold: the University of California annual, class of 1893.* San Francisco, 1892. p.46-49. (Unsigned) Norris also contributed the illustrations on p.50, 51, and 231 of this volume.
153. Clothes of steel. *San Francisco Chronicle* March 31, 1889, p.6. (Unsigned) Norris' first published work. In various sources, this article has been cited as "Ancient armour."
154. College athletics. *Wave* 15,no.50:13 December 12, 1896.
155. A College man as a feature of San Francisco society. *Wave* 16,no.1:3 January 2, 1897. (Unsigned)
156. *Comida:* an experience in famine. *Atlantic Monthly* 83:343-48 March 1899.
157. Cosmopolitan San Francisco. *Wave* 16,no.52:4 December 25, 1897 (Christmas supplement).

158. The Coverfield sweepstakes. *Occident* 19,no.11:145-47 December 19, 1890. (Signed "Norrys")
159. Crane in London. *Wave* 16,no.38:13 September 18, 1897. (Signed "Justin Sturgis")
160. The cruiser Hi-Yei. *Wave* 16,no.27:5 July 3, 1897.
161. Dago conspirators. *Wave* 16,no.38:7 September 18, 1897. (Signed "Justin Sturgis")
162. A day with the University of California team. *Wave* 15,no.46:6 November 14, 1896.
163. The decline of the magazine short story. *Wave* 16,no.5:3 January 30, 1897. (Unsigned)
164. A delayed masterpiece. *Wave* 15,no.17:8 April 25, 1896. (Unsigned) A review of Elizabeth Stuart Phelps' *The singular life.*
165. Election night on a daily. *Wave* 15,no.45:7 November 7, 1896.
166. The English courses in the University of California. *Wave* 15,no.48:2-3 November 28, 1896. (Unsigned)
167. Ethics of the freshman rush. *Wave* 16,no.36:2 September 4, 1897. (Unsigned)
168. Evolution of a freshman. *Wave* 16,no.34:8-9 August 21, 1897. (Unsigned)
169. The evolution of a nurse. *Wave* 15,no.42:8 October 17, 1896.
170. Fiction in review. *Wave* 15,no.29:12 July 18, 1896. A review of Maria Louise Pool's *In a dike shanty,* Sara Jeanette Duncan's *His Honour, and a lady,* and Arthur Morrison's *Chronicles of Martin Hewitt.*
171. Fiction is selection. *Wave* 16,no.37:3 September 11, 1897. (Signed "Justin Sturgis")
172. Fiction writing as a business. *Boston Evening Tran-*

script January 1, 1902, p.17.

173. The frantic rush from Johannesburg. *San Francisco Chronicle* March 1, 1896, p.8. Illustrated with pen-and-ink sketches by Norris.
174. Frawley's new beauty; an impression of the opinions of Miss Gladys Wallis. *Wave* 16,no.22:11 May 29, 1897.
175. From Cape Town to Kimberley Mine. *San Francisco Chronicle* January 26, 1896, p.1. Illustrated with pen-and-ink sketches by Norris.
176. From field to storehouse. *Wave* 16,no.32:6 August 7, 1897. (Unsigned)
177. The frontier gone at last. *World's Work* 3:1728-31 February 1902.
178. The "Great American novelist." Syndicated January 19, 1903. Newspaper appearance not verified.
179. The happenings of Jones. *Wave* 17,no.7:6 February 12, 1898. (Signed "Justin Sturgis")
180. Happiness by conquest. *Wave* 16,no.50:2 December 11, 1897.
181. History of the class of '94. *Blue and gold: the University of California annual, class of 1894.* San Francisco, 1893. p.28-29. (Unsigned) Norris also contributed the illustrations on p.81, 114, 133, 155, 194, and 246 of this volume.
182. Holiday literature. *Wave* 16,no.50:8 December 11, 1897. (Unsigned)
183. The Hopkins Institute: art education in San Francisco. *Wave* 16,no.39:9 September 25, 1897. (Signed "Justin Sturgis")
184. How it strikes the observer: the horse show. *Wave* 15,no.50:7 December 12, 1896.
185. Hunting human game. *Wave* 16,no.4:4 January 23, 1897.

186. Imitators of Noah. *Wave* 16,no.26:8 June 26, 1897. (Unsigned)
187. In defense of Doctor W. Lawlor. *Argonaut* 51:87 August 11, 1902. A letter dated August 6, 1902, originally entitled "Frank Norris defends Dr. Lawlor."
188. In the compound of a diamond mine. *San Francisco Chronicle* February 2, 1896, p.10. Illustrated with pen-and-ink sketches by Norris.
189. In the veldt of the Transvaal. *San Francisco Chronicle* February 9, 1896, p.1. Illustrated with pen-and-ink sketch by Norris.
190. Inside an organ. *Wave* 16,no.1:9 January 2, 1897.
191. Italy in California. *Wave* 15,no.43:9 October 24, 1896.
192. Jack Hammond in Johannesburg and Pretoria. *Wave* 15,no.25:5 June 20, 1896.
193. Lackaye "making-up." *Wave* 15,no.49:4 December 5, 1896. An interview with Wilton Lackaye.
194. A "lag's" release. *Wave* 16,no.13:4 March 27, 1897.
195. Life in the mining region. *Everybody's Magazine* 7:241-48 September 1902.
196. Literature of the West: a reply to William R. Lighton. *Boston Evening Transcript* January 8, 1902, p.17. Reprinted: *American Literature* 8:190-98 May 1936; see item 437.
197. The making of a pianiste. *Wave* 15,no.46:5 November 14, 1896.
198. The making of a statue. *Wave* 16,no.7:4 February 13, 1897.
199. Man hunting. *Wave* 15,no.24:8 June 13, 1896. (Unsigned)
200. The marriage problem. *Wave* 16,no.26:7 June 26, 1897. (Signed "Justin Sturgis")

201. Maud Odell and Zenda. *Wave* 15,no.42:8 October 17, 1896.
202. The mechanics of fiction. *Boston Evening Transcript* December 4, 1901, p.22.
203. Metropolitan noises. *Wave* 16,no.21:9 May 22, 1897. (Unsigned)
204. Millard's tales. *Wave* 16,no.34:12 August 21, 1897. A review of F. B. Millard's *A pretty bandit.*
205. A miner interviewed. *Wave* 16,no.30:11 July 24, 1897.
206. The Mira Monte club. *Wave* 16,no.49:3 December 4, 1897.
207. Miss Sabel's husband. *Wave* 16,no.27:11 July 3, 1897.
208. Mr. Kipling's 'Kim.' *World's Work* 2:1341-42 September 1901. (Unsigned)
209. Mrs. Carter at home. *Wave* 16,no.33:6 August 14, 1897. An interview with Mrs. Leslie Carter.
210. Monsieur LeRoy explains. *Wave* 16,no.52:11 December 25, 1897. (Signed "Justin Sturgis")
211. Moving a fifty-ton gun. *Wave* 15,no.45:5 November 7, 1896.
212. The national spirit as it relates to the "Great American novel." *Boston Evening Transcript* February 5, 1902, p.11. Reprinted: *American Literature* 8:190-98 May 1936; see item 437.
213. The nature revival in literature. Syndicated February 16, 1903. Newspaper appearance not verified.
214. The need of a literary conscience. *World's Work* 3:1559-60 December 1901.
215. A neglected epic; how the real hero of the American westward movement has been forgotten in literature. *World's Work* 5:2904-06 December 1902.

216. New Year's at San Quentin. *Wave* 16,no.2:8 January 9, 1897.
217. New York as a literary centre. Syndicated January 19, 1902. Newspaper appearance not verified.
218. The newest books. *Wave* 16,no.31:13 July 31, 1897.
219. Newspaper criticisms and American fiction. Syndicated March 9, 1903. Newspaper appearance not verified.
220. The novel with a "purpose." *World's Work* 4:2117-19 May 1902.
221. Novelists of the future; the training they need. *Boston Evening Transcript* November 27, 1901, p.14.
222. Novelists to order—while you wait. Syndicated February 23, 1903. Newspaper appearance not verified.
223. On a battleship. *Wave* 15,no.42:7 October 17, 1896.
224. One kind of a new woman. *Wave* 16,no.5:6 January 30, 1897.
225. An opening for novelists; great opportunities for fiction writers in San Francisco. *Wave* 16,no.21:7 May 22, 1897.
226. The opinions of Leander. A series of sketches including the following: 'Holds forth at length on the subject of girl. *Wave* 16,no.29:7 July 17, 1897; 'Holdeth forth upon our boys and the ways of them. *Wave* 16,no.30:7 July 24, 1897; 'Commenteth at length upon letters received. *Wave* 16,no.31:5 July 31, 1897; 'Falleth from grace and subsequently from a springboard. *Wave* 16,no.32:5 August 7, 1897; Showing the plausible mistake of a misguided Eastern man. *Wave* 16,no.33:13 August 14, 1897; Opinions of Justin Sturgis by Leander. *Wave* 16,no.34:13 August 21, 1897.

227. Passing of "Little Pete." *Wave* 16,no.5:7 January 30, 1897.
228. Perverted tales. *Wave* 16,no.52:5-7 December 25, 1897 (Christmas supplement). Parodies of several well-known authors: "The 'ricksha that happened" by R—d K—g; "The green stone of unrest" by S—n Cr—e; "Van Bubble's story" by R—d H—g D—s; "Ambrosia Beer" by A—e B—e; "I call on Lady Dotty" by An—y H—pe; "A hero of Tomato Can" by B—t H—te.
229. Pictures to burn. *Wave* 16,no.18:4 May 1, 1897. (Signed "Justin Sturgis")
230. A plea for romantic fiction. *Boston Evening Transcript* December 18, 1901, p.14.
231. The postal telegraph. *Wave* 16,no.51:20 December 18, 1897. (Unsigned)
232. A problem in fiction: truth versus accuracy. *Boston Evening Transcript* November 6, 1901, p.20.
233. Pseudo-architecture. *Wave* 16,no.24:6 June 12, 1897. (Signed "Justin Sturgis")
234. The question. *Wave* 16,no.25:13 June 19, 1897. (Unsigned)
235. A question of ideals. *Wave* 15,no.52:7 December 26, 1896.
236. Re-creating a university. *Wave* 15,no.44:5 October 31, 1896.
237. Responsibilities of the novelist. *Critic* 41:537-40 December 1902.
238. Retail bookseller—literary dictator. *Boston Evening Transcript* November 20, 1901, p.20.
239. Reviews in brief. *Wave* 16,no.52:12 December 25, 1897.
240. Rhodes and the reporters. *Wave* 15,no.15:5 April 11, 1896.

241. Richard Harding Davis. Syndicated January 26, 1903. Listed in *Gaer,* but newspaper appearance not verified and text not reprinted.
242. Sailing of the *Excelsior*. *Wave* 16,no.31:7 July 31, 1897.
243. Salt and sincerity. *Critic* 40:447-50, 550-55; 41:77-81, 178-82, 267-70, 363-67 May-October 1902.
244. Santa Cruz Venetian carnival. *Wave* 15,no.26:8 June 27, 1896.
245. The scoop. *Wave* 16,no.13:6 March 27, 1897. (Signed "Justin Sturgis")
246. Simplicity in art. *Boston Evening Transcript* Janary 15, 1902, p.17.
247. The Sketch Club exhibit. *Wave* 15,no.48:9 November 28, 1896.
248. A south sea expedition. *Wave* 16,no.8:8 February 20, 1897.
249. The stage and California girls. *Wave* 15,no.25:8 June 20, 1896.
250. The Stanford eleven at home. *Wave* 15,no.47:6 November 21, 1896.
251. Stephen Crane's stories of life in the slums. *Wave* 15,no.27:13 July 4, 1896. A review of Crane's *Maggie* and *George's mother.*
252. Stepterfetchit, by Dick Wincey. *Occident* 20,no.7:79 March 27, 1891.
253. Stepterfetchit, by Karl Aisle. *Occident* 20,no.8:86 April 3, 1891.
254. Stepterfetchit, by 'Mick' Aulay. *Occident* 20,no.9: 104 April 10, 1891.
255. Story-tellers vs. novelists. *World's Work* 3:1894-97 March 1902.
256. A strange relief ship. *Wave* 16,no.24:7 June 12, 1897. (Unsigned)

257. Street scenes in Johannesburg during the insurrection of January 1896. *Harper's Weekly* 40:233 March 7, 1896.
258. Student life in Paris. *Collier's Weekly* 25:33 May 12, 1900.
259. Suggestions (I. 1870; II. A hotel bedroom; III. Brute; IV. The dental parlors). *Wave* 16,no.11:7 March 13, 1897.
260. A summer in Arcady. *Wave* 15,no.30:9 July 25, 1896.
261. The surrender of Santiago. *New York Sun* July 13, 1913, section 7, p.1-2.
262. A tale and the truth. *Wave* 16,no.39:14 September 25, 1897.
263. Theory and reality. *Wave* 15,no.18:8 May 2, 1896. A review of William Dean Howells' *A parting and a meeting* and Mrs. J. R. Jarboe's *Robert Atterbury.*
264. Thomas on tendencies. *Wave* 16,no.38:5 September 18, 1897.
265. Training of firemen. *Wave* 16,no.24:9 June 12, 1897.
266. Trilby and Princess Flavia. *Wave* 15,no.41:8 October 10, 1896.
267. The true reward of the novelist. *World's Work* 2:1337-39 October 1901.
268. Types of Western men: the college man. (Types of Western men, I). *Wave* 15,no.17:6 April 25, 1896. (Signed "Marmaduke Masters")
269. The University of California track team. *Wave* 16,no.6:4 February 6, 1897.
270. The unknown author and the publisher. *World's Work* 1:663-65 April 1901. (Signed "A publisher's reader")

271. The upper office at work. *Wave* 16,no.31:4-5 July 31, 1897.
272. Virtue and actresses. *Wave* 17,no.2:6 January 8, 1898. (Signed "Justin Sturgis")
273. The "volunteer manuscript." *Boston Evening Transcript* December 11, 1901, p.25. Reprinted: *The author's yearbook for 1902.* New York, Booklover press, 1902. p.24-34.
274. Waiting for their cue. *Wave* 15,no.50:9 December 12, 1896.
275. The week's football. *Wave* 15,no.42:11 October 17, 1896; 15,no.43:13 October 24, 1896; 15,no.44:13 October 31, 1896; 15,no.45:13 November 7, 1896; 15,no.46:13 November 14, 1896; 15,no.47:13 November 21, 1896; 15,no.48:11 November 28, 1896.
276. Western city types. A series of sketches including the following: The plumber's apprentice. *Wave* 15,no.18:6 May 2, 1896; The "fast girl." *Wave* 15,no.19:5 May 9, 1896; An art student. *Wave* 15,no.20:10 May 16, 1896. (Item 268, "Types of Western men: the college man" is related to this series.)
277. When a woman hesitates. *Wave* 16,no.22:5 May 29, 1897.
278. Where tamales are made. *Wave* 16,no.3:9 January 16, 1897.
279. Why women should write the best novels—and why they don't. *Boston Evening Transcript* November 13, 1901, p.20.
280. With Lawton at El Caney. *Century Magazine* 58(n.s.36):304-09 June 1899.
281. Zola as a romantic writer. *Wave* 15,no.26:3 June 27, 1896. (Unsigned)

282. A Zulu war dance. *San Francisco Chronicle* March 15, 1896, p.1. Illustrated with pen-and-ink sketches by Norris.

Translations

283. An elopement. Translated from the French of Ferdinand Bloch. *Wave* 16,no.52:13 December 25, 1897.
284. Fifi. Translated from the French of Léon Faran. *Wave* 16,no.4:5 January 23, 1897.
285. Not guilty. Translated from the French of Marcel L'Heureux. *Wave* 16,no.25:5 June 19, 1897. (Signed "Justin Sturgis")
286. The story of a wall. Translated from the French of Pierre Loti. *Wave* 16,no.35:13 August 28, 1897.

PART II

WRITINGS ABOUT FRANK NORRIS

Books, Parts of Books, & Periodical Articles

287. Adams, James Donald. "Winds for the sail," in his *The shape of books to come.* New York, Viking, 1944. p.49-52.

288. Åhnebrink, Lars. *The beginnings of naturalism in American fiction; a study of the works of Hamlin Garland, Stephen Crane, and Frank Norris, with special reference to some European influences, 1891-1903.* Upsala, Lundequistska bokhandeln; Cambridge, Harvard University press [1950] 505p. (Upsala. Universitet. Amerikanska seminariet. Essays and studies on American language and literature. 9)

289. ——*The influence of Émile Zola on Frank Norris.* Upsala, Lundequistska bokhandeln; Cambridge, Harvard University press [1947] 68p. (Essays and studies on American language and literature. 5)

290. [Aiken, Charles Sedgwick] "Books and writers," *Sunset* 10:245 January 1903.

291. Altenbernd, August Lynn. *The intellectual currents in* The octopus: *a study of the naturalism of Frank Norris.* Unpublished M.A. thesis, Ohio State University, 1949. 88p. (Abstract in Ohio State University *Abstracts of masters' theses* no.-61:5, 1951)

292. Anderson, Grace E. *A dictionary of characters in the novels of Frank Norris.* Unpublished M.A. thesis, University of Kansas, 1933. 123p.

293. Armes, William Dallam. "Concerning the work of the late Frank Norris," *Sunset* 10:165-67 December 1902.

294. Baeckelmans, Lode. "Amerikaansche letteren... [Frank Norris]" *Bibliotheekgids* 4,no.10:175-76

December 1925.

295. Beach, Joseph Warren. *The twentieth century novel.* New York, Appleton-Century-Crofts [c1932] p.322.

296. Bechter, Leslie G. *Frank Norris: his place in the development of the American novel.* Unpublished M.A. thesis, State University of Iowa, 1939. 86p.

297. Beer, Thomas. *The mauve decade.* New York, Alfred A. Knopf, 1926. passim.

298. Benét, William Rose. "Rereading *The pit*," *Saturday Review of Literature* 25:17 July 25, 1942.

299. Beranek, Henriette. *Das "Gilded Age" im Romanwerk des Frank Norris.* Ph.D. dissertation, University of Vienna, 1951. 125p. [Maschinenschrift]

300. Berg, Ruben Gustafsson. *Moderna Amerikaner.* Stockholm, H. Gebers [1925] p.182-84.

301. Biencourt, Marius. *Une influence du naturalisme français en Amérique: Frank Norris.* Paris, Giard, 1933. 244p. (Thesis, University of Paris)

302. "Biographical sketch of Frank Norris," *Book News* 21:443 February 1903.

303. Bixler, Paul H. "Frank Norris's literary reputation," *American Literature* 6:109-21 May 1934.

304. Blankenship, Russell. *American literature as an expression of the national mind.* New York, Henry Holt [1935] p.527-32.

305. Boas, Ralph Philip. *Social backgrounds of American literature.* Boston, Little, Brown, 1933. p.185-87.

306. "The book and the public," *Town Talk* (San Francisco) 9,no.455:24-25 May 18, 1901.

307. Boynton, Percy Holmes. *The rediscovery of the frontier.* Chicago, University of Chicago Press [c1931] p.77-79.

308. Britten, Florence Haxton. " 'Prissy' Frank Norris." *New York Herald Tribune Books,* August 23, 1931, p.13.
309. Brooks, Van Wyck. "Frank Norris and Jack London," in his *The confident years: 1885-1915.* New York, Dutton, 1952. p.217-36 and passim.
310. —— *Sketches in criticism.* New York, Dutton [c1932] p.173-74.
311. Brown, Deming Bronson. *The development of the use of symbolism in the novels of Frank Norris.* Unpublished M.A. thesis, University of Washington, 1942. 91p. (Abstract in University of Washington. *Abstracts of theses* 8:27 June 1944)
312. Bruns, Friedrich. "Naturalismus. Die Anfange: Hamlin Garland. Stephen Crane. Frank Norris. Jack London," in his *Die amerikanische Dichtung der Gegenwart.* Berlin and Leipzig, Teubner, 1930. p.18-22.
313. Burgess, Frank Gelett. "One more tribute to Frank Norris," *Sunset* 10:246 January 1903.
314. Calverton, Victor Francis. *The liberation of American literature.* New York, Scribner's, 1932. p.350-54.
315. Cargill, Oscar. *Intellectual America.* New York, Macmillan, 1941. p.89-107 and passim.
316. Chamberlain, John. *Farewell to reform.* New York, Liveright [c1932] p.107.
317. —— "The 'prentice days of Frank Norris." *New York Times Book Review* May 3, 1931, p.2, 10.
318. Chamberlin, William Fosdick. *The history of Phi Gamma Delta.* New York, The fraternity, 1926. v.2, passim.
319. Chase, Richard Volney. "Norris and naturalism,"

in his *The American novel and its tradition.* Garden City, N.Y., Doubleday, 1957. p.185-204.

320. Chislett, William. *Moderns and near moderns; essays on Henry James, Stockton, Shaw, and others.* New York, Grafton Press [c1928] p.109-11, 116-20.

321. Clarke, Robert Montgomery. *Contemporary American novelists: Frank Norris.* Unpublished M.A. thesis, Stanford University, 1932. 120p.

322. Clift, Denison Hailey. "The artist in Frank Norris," *Pacific Monthly* 17:313-22 March 1907.

323. Cooper, Frederic Taber. "Frank Norris," *Bookman* (N.Y.) 16:334-35 December 1902.

324. —— "Frank Norris, realist," *Bookman* (N.Y.) 10:234-38 November 1899.

325. —— "Frank Norris's *The octopus,*" *Bookman* (N.Y) 13:245-47 May 1901.

326. —— *Some American story tellers.* New York, Henry Holt, 1911. p.295-330.

327. —— "The sustained effort and some recent novels," *Bookman* (N.Y.) 18:309-14 November 1903.

328. Cowley, Malcolm. "Naturalism's terrible McTeague," *New Republic* 116:31-33 May 5, 1947.

329. —— " 'Not men': a natural history of American naturalism," *Kenyon Review* 9:414-35 Summer 1947.

330. Crane, Maurice A. "The case of the drunken goldfish," *College English* 17:309-10 February 1956.

331. Crane, Warren Eugene. *The life and works of Frank Norris as a reflection of historical and literary trends between 1890 and 1902.* Unpublished M.A. thesis, University of Washington, 1939. 88p. (Abstract in University of Washington. *Bulletin,* Theses series, 5:68-70 May 1941)

332. Davenport, Eleanor M. "Frank Norris," *The U.C. Magazine* (University of California) 3,no.7:80-82 November 1897.
333. "Death ends the career of Frank Norris," *San Francisco Chronicle* October 26, 1902, p.24.
334. "The death of Mr. Frank Norris," *World's Work* 5:2830 December 1902.
335. "Death stills the pen of Frank Norris and ends career of a literary genius," *San Francisco Examiner* October 26, 1902, p.18.
336. Dell, Floyd. "Chicago in fiction," *Bookman* (N.Y.) 38:270-74 November 1913.
337. Dickinson, Thomas H. *The making of American literature.* New York, Century [c1932] p.645-46.
338. Dobie, Charles Caldwell. "Frank Norris, or up from culture," *American Mercury* 13:412-24 April 1928.
339. Dreiser, Theodore. "The early adventures of Sister Carrie," *Colophon* pt. 5, February 1931, p[4]
340. —— *Letters . . . a selection.* Edited by Robert H. Elias. Philadelphia, University of Pennsylvania Press [1959] 3v. passim.
341. Duffus, R. L. "Norris in retrospect," *New York Times Book Review* June 8, 1947, p.5.
342. Dusha, Ruth Anne. *Some sociological realists in American fiction in the nineteenth century.* Unpublished M.A. thesis, Columbia University, 1931. 112p.
343. East, Harry M. "A lesson from Frank Norris," *Overland Monthly* 60:533-34 December 1912.
344. Edgar, Randolph. "Frank Benjamin Franklin Norris, 1870-1902," *Publishers' Weekly* 103:637 March 3, 1923. (A bibliographic checklist)
345. —— "The revival of Frank Norris," *Boston Evening Transcript* May 3, 1930, p.1-2.

346. Edmondson, Elsie Fannie Louise. *The writer as hero in important American fiction since Howells.* Ph.D. dissertation, University of Michigan, 1954. 274p. (Abstract in *Dissertation Abstracts* 14:1077-78, 1954. University Microfilms publication no.8297)

347. Eldredge, Zoeth Skinner. *History of California.* New York, Century History Company [1915] v.5, p.498-99.

348. Everett, Wallace W. "Frank Norris in his chapter," *Phi Gamma Delta Magazine* 52:561-66 April 1930.

349. Fischer, Walther Paul. *Amerikanische Prosa vom Bürgerkrieg bis auf die Gegenwart (1863-1922).* Leipzig, Berlin, Teubner, 1926. p.57-59.

350. —— *Die englische Literatur de Vereinigten Staaten von Nordamerika.* Wildpark-Potsdam, Akademische Verlagsgesellschaft Athenaion m.b.h. [1929] (Handbuch der Literaturwissenschaft. Lief.131, 136, 147, 154) p.113.

351. Flower, B. O. "The trust in fiction: a remarkable social novel," *Arena* 27:547-54 May 1902.

352. "Frank Norris," *Literary News* 24:9-10 January 1903.

353. "Frank Norris; an appreciation," *New York Herald,* Literary section, March 1, 1903, p.2.

354. "Frank Norris on the responsibilities of the novelist," *Literary Digest* 25:831-32 December 20, 1902. (Summarizes items 215 and 237)

355. "Frank Norris's last work," *Argonaut* 51:289-90 November 10, 1902.

356. "Frank Norris's werewolf," *Current Opinion* 56: 455-56 June 1914.

357. French, John C. "Norris, Benjamin Franklin," *Dictionary of American biography.* New York, Scribners, 1928. v.13, p.551-52.
358. "From one who knows," *Town Talk* (San Francisco) 10,no.513:26 June 28, 1902.
359. Fullerton, Bradford Morton. *A selective bibliography of American literature, 1775-1900.* New York, William Farquhar Payson, 1932. p.206.
360. Gaer, Joseph. *Frank Norris (Benjamin Franklin Norris) bibliography and biographical data.* [n.p., 1934] 50p. ([California literary research project] Monograph 3) Mimeographed.
361. Garland, Hamlin. *Companions on the trail; a literary chronicle.* New York, Macmillan, 1931. p.166-71.
362. —— "The work of Frank Norris," *Critic* 42:216-18 March 1903.
363. Garnett, Edward. *Friday nights.* New York, Knopf, 1922. p.295-96.
364. Geismar, Maxwell David. "Frank Norris: and the brute," in his *Rebels and ancestors.* Boston, Houghton Mifflin, 1953. p.3-66.
365. [Gilder, Jeanette] [Editorial signed "The Lounger"] *Critic* 34(n.s.31):398 May 1899.
366. —— [Editorial signed "The Lounger"] *Putnam's Magazine* 6:629-33 August 1909.
367. Ghodes, Clarence Louis Frank. "Facts of life versus pleasant reading," in Quinn, Arthur Hobson, ed., *The literature of the American people.* New York, Appleton-Century-Crofts [1951] p.737-62.
368. Goldsmith, Arnold Louis. *Free will, determinism, and social responsibility in the writings of Oliver Wendell Holmes, Sr., Frank Norris, and Henry*

James. Unpublished Ph.D. dissertation, University of Wisconsin, 1953. 390p. (Abstract in Wisconsin. University. *Summaries of doctoral dissertations* 15:610-12, 1955)

368a.——"The development of Frank Norris's philosophy," in Wayne State University. Dept. of English. *Studies in honor of John Wilcox.* Detroit, Wayne State University press, 1958. p.175-94.

369. Goodrich, Arthur. "Frank Norris," *Current Literature* 33:764 December 1902.

370. —— "Frank Norris; the estimate and tribute of an associate," *Boston Evening Transcript* October 29, 1902, p.14.

371. —— "Frank Norris, the man," *Current Literature* 34:105 January 1903.

372. Grattan, C. Hartley. "Frank Norris," *Bookman* (N.Y.) 69:506-10 July 1929.

373. —— "Frank Norris," *Nation* 135:535-36 November 30, 1932.

374. Haney, John Louis. *The story of our literature.* New York, Scribner's, 1923. passim.

375. Harrison, Robert. *The writings of Frank Norris as viewed by his contemporaries.* Unpublished M.A. thesis, Ohio University (Athens), 1941. 52p. (Abstract in Ohio University (Athens). *Abstracts of masters' theses,* 1941, p.32)

376. Hart, James D. "Search and research: the librarian and the scholar," *College and Research Libraries* 19:365-74 September 1958. (The section dealing with Norris was reprinted in the Book Club of California. *News-Letter* 24,no.2:27-34 Spring 1959)

377. Hartwick, Harry. "Norris and the brute," in his *The foreground of American fiction.* New York,

American Book Company [c1934] p.45-66 and passim.

378. Hatcher, Harlan. *Creating the modern American novel.* New York, Farrar and Rinehart [c1935] p.15-18.

379. Hazard, Lucy Lockwood. *The frontier in American literature.* New York, Barnes and Noble, 1941. p.267-69.

380. Hellman, Geoffrey. "Trail-blazer of realism," *New York Herald Tribune Books* December 4, 1932, p.25.

381. Hellström, Gustaf. " 'Vilda västern' i Nyare Amerikansk litteratur," *Vår tid; årsbok utgiven av samfundet de Nio* (Stockholm) 10:47-91 1925.

382. Hicks, Granville. *The great tradition.* New York, Macmillan, 1933. p.168-75 and passim.

383. Hill, Marion V. *A study of thematic forces in the novels of Frank Norris.* Unpublished M.A. thesis, Bowling Green State University, 1954. 62p. (Abstract in Ohio. State University, Bowling Green. *Abstracts of masters' theses (1953-54)* 5:48-49, 1955)

384. Hinkel, Edgar J. *Criticism of California literature.* Oakland, Calif., Alameda County Public Library, 1940. v.2, p.669-97.

385. Hoffman, Charles G. "Norris and the responsibility of the novelist," *South Atlantic Quarterly* 54:508-15 October 1955.

386. Houston, Margaret Dorothy. *Frank Norris' theory of romanticism and its application in* The octopus. Unpublished M.A. thesis, University of Washington, 1939. 75p. (Abstract in University of Washington. *Bulletin,* Theses series, 5:74-77 May 1941)

387. Howard, Eric. "Frank Norris," in Hunt, Rockwell Dennis, ed. *California and Californians.* Chicago, New York, Lewis Publishing Company, 1930. v.4, p.89-90.
388. Howells, William Dean. "American letter; some recent novels," *Literature* 3:577-79 December 17, 1898.
389. —— "A case in point," *Literature* n.s.1:241-42 March 24, 1899.
390. —— "Editor's easy chair," *Harper's Monthly* 103: 824-25 October 1901; 106:328 January 1903.
391. —— "Frank Norris," *North American Review* 175: 769-78 December 1902.
392. —— "Last work of Frank Norris," *Harper's Weekly* 47:433 March 14, 1903.
393. —— *The life in letters of William Dean Howells,* edited by Mildred Howells. Garden City, Doubleday, Doran, 1928. v.2, p.102-03. (Includes a letter from Norris to Howells)
394. "In memoriam (Frank Norris memorial chair)," *University of California Chronicle* 16:453 October 1914.
395. Jensen, Johannes V. "Frank Norris: The octopus!" *März* 1,pt.2:67-73 April 1907.
396. Kaplan, Charles. "Fact into fiction in *McTeague,*" *Harvard Library Bulletin* 8:381-85 Autumn 1954.
397. —— *Frank Norris and the craft of fiction.* Unpublished Ph.D. dissertation, Northwestern University, 1952. 332p. (Abstract in Northwestern University. *Summaries of doctoral dissertations* 20:19-24, 1952)
398. —— "Norris's use of sources in *The pit,*" *American Literature* 25:75-84 March 1953.

399. Kazin, Alfred. *On native grounds.* New York, Reynal and Hitchcock, [1942] p.97-102 and passim.

400. —— "Three pioneer realists," *Saturday Review of Literature* 20:3-4, 14-15 July 8, 1939.

401. Kellner, Leon. *Geschichte der nordamerikanischen Literatur.* Berlin, Göschen, 1913. v.1, p.19; v.2, p.89.

402. —— *American literature* . . . translated from the German by Julia Franklin. Garden City, Doubleday, Page, 1915. p.23-24.

403. Kerst, Henri. "Romanciers américains contemporains," in *Cahiers des langues modernes.* I. Paris, Librairie Didier [1946] p.31-32 and passim.

404. Klein, Karl-Heinz. *Frank Norris' Erzählungswerk im Verhältnis zu seiner Kunsttheorie.* Ph.D. dissertation, University of Marburg, 1952. 143p. [Maschinenschrift]

405. Knight, Grant Cochran. *American literature and culture.* New York, Long and Smith, 1932. p.389-95.

406. —— *The novel in English.* New York, R. R. Smith, 1931. p.298-303.

407. —— *Superlatives.* New York, Knopf, 1925. p.119-21.

408. —— "Victory of realism," in his *The critical period in American literature.* Chapel Hill, University of North Carolina Press [1951] p.161-68 and passim.

409. Kranendonk, Anthonius Gerardus van. *Geschiedenis van de amerikaanse literatur.* Amsterdam, G. A. van Oorschot, 1946. v.1, p.310-12.

410. Kusler, Gerald E. *The evolution of Frank Norris as a novelist.* Unpublished M.A. thesis, State University of Iowa, 1950. 143p.

411. Kwiat, Joseph J. "Frank Norris: the novelist as social critic and literary theorist," *Die Neuren Sprachen* n.f.3,heft 9:385-92 1954.
412. —— "The newspaper experience: Crane, Norris, and Dreiser," *Nineteenth Century Fiction* 8:99-117 September 1953.
413. Leisy, Ernest Erwin. *American literature; an interpretative survey.* New York, Crowell [c1929] p.207-08.
414. Letizia, Louise M. *Frank Norris: a study in contrasts and contradictions.* Unpublished M.A. thesis, University of Pittsburgh, 1950. 98p.
415. Levick, Milne B. "Frank Norris," *Overland Monthly* n.s.45:504-08 June 1905.
416. Lewis, Oscar. "Frank Norris' California locale," *Hesperian* Winter 1930 (unpaged).
417. Lewisohn, Ludwig. *Expressionism in America.* New York, Harper, 1932. p.322-27 and passim.
418. Loggins, Vernon. "Dominant primordial," in his *I hear America.* New York, Crowell [c1937] p.113-25 and passim.
419. Logue, Charles William. *Frank Norris: a study in romantic realism.* Unpublished M.A. thesis, St. John's University, 1949. 94p. (Abstract in St. John's University. *Abstracts of dissertations* 4:59-60, 1949/50)
420. Lummis, Charles F. "In Western letters," *Out West* 13:18 June 1900.
421. Lundy, Robert Donald. *The making of* McTeague *and* The octopus. Unpublished Ph.D. dissertation, University of California (Berkeley), 1956. 333p. (Abstract in California. University. Graduate Division. *Programmes of final examinations,* 1956)

422. Lynn, Kenneth Schuyler. "Frank Norris: mama's boy," in his *Dream of success; a study of the modern American imagination.* Boston, Little, Brown [1955] p.158-207.

423. McCole, C. John. *Lucifer at large.* London, New York, Longmans, Green, 1937. p.24-26.

424. McCormick, Paul S. *Frank Norris and the American epic.* Unpublished M.A. thesis, Columbia University, 1931. 42p.

425. McGinn, Richard Joseph. *The characterization of women in the novels of Frank Norris.* Unpublished M.A. thesis, Columbia University, 1954. 100p.

426. McKee, Irving. "Notable memorials to Mussel Slough," *Pacific Historical Review* 17:19-27 February 1948.

427. Macy, John Albert. *American writers on American literature.* New York, H. Liveright [c1931] passim.

428. Mahin, Sarah Jane. *Formative influences on Frank Norris's novel* McTeague. Unpublished M.A. thesis, University of Iowa, 1944. 95p.

429. Marchand, Ernest LeRoy. *Frank Norris: a study.* Ph.D. dissertation, University of Wisconsin, 1938. 426p. (Abstract in Wisconsin. University. *Summaries of doctoral dissertations* 4:232-34 1940)

430. —— *Frank Norris, a study.* Stanford, Stanford University Press; London, H. Milford, Oxford University Press [1942] 258p.

431. Marcosson, Isaac Frederick. *Adventures in interviewing.* London, John Lane, The Bodley Head; New York, John Lane, 1920. p.232-41 and passim.

432. —— *Before I forget.* New York, Dodd, Mead, 1959. p.500-08 and passim.

433. Markham, Edwin. *California, the wonderful.* New York, Hearst's International Library Company [c1914] p.363.
434. —— *Songs and stories.* San Francisco, Powell [c1931] v.8 (California), p.15-16.
435. Martin, Willard E. "The establishment of the order of printings in books printed from plates: illustrated in Frank Norris's *The octopus*," *American Literature* 5:17-28 March 1933.
436. —— "Frank Norris's reading at Harvard College," *American Literature* 7:203-04 May 1935.
437. —— "Two uncollected essays by Frank Norris," *American Literature* 8:190-98 May 1936. (Reprints "Literature of the West" and "The national spirit as it relates to the 'Great American novel' ")
438. Matthews, Margaret Moore. *Frank Norris: pioneer realist.* Unpublished M.A. thesis, University of South Carolina, 1937. 51p.
439. Matthiessen, Francis Otto. *Theodore Dreiser.* New York, William Sloane, 1951. p.58-59 and passim.
440. "Memories of Frank Norris," *Bookman* (N.Y.) 39:236-38 May 1914.
441. Mencken, Henry Louis. *A book of prefaces.* New York, Knopf, 1917. p.70-71.
442. Meyer, George Wilbur. "A new interpretation of *The octopus*," *College English* 4:351-59 March 1943.
443. Michaud, Regis. *Panorama de la littérature américaine contemporaine.* Paris, Kra [c1928] p.139-41.
444. Mighels, Ella Sterling Cummins. *The story of the files.* [San Francisco, Co-operative Printing Company, c1893] p.359-60.
445. Millard, Bailey. "A significant literary life," *Out*

West 18:49-55 January 1903.

446. Mitchell, Marvin O'Neill. *A study of realistic and romantic elements in the fiction of E. W. Howe, Joseph Kirkland, Hamlin Garland, Harold Frederic, and Frank Norris (1882-1902).* Unpublished Ph.D. dissertation, University of North Carolina, 1953. 488p. (Abstract in University of North Carolina. *Record* no.534:95-96 January-December 1953)
447. Morley, S. A. "Frank Norris, American realist," *Trek* 11,no.15:16 January 24, 1947.
448. Morris, Ethiel Virginia. *Frank Norris' trilogy on American life.* Unpublished M.A. thesis, University of Kansas, 1928. 102p.
449. Muller, Herbert Joseph. *Modern fiction.* New York, Funk and Wagnalls [1937] p.201-02.
450. Norris, Charles Gilman. *Frank Norris.* [New York] Doubleday, Page [1914] 28p.
451. "Norris died intestate," *San Francisco Chronicle* November 7, 1902, p.14.
452. O'Connor, William Van. *An age of criticism: 1900-1950.* Chicago, H. Regnery, 1952. p.41-42.
453. O'Dell, Barry. "Recollecting Frank Norris," *San Franciscan* 5,no.2:12, 36 December 1930.
454. Overton, Grant. *An hour of the American novel.* Philadelphia and London, J. B. Lippincott, 1929. p.109-11.
455. Pallette, Drew B. *The theories and practice of Frank Norris as related to his California background.* Unpublished M.A. thesis, University of Southern California, 1934. 105p.
456. Parrington, Vernon Louis. "The development of realism," in Foerster, Norman. *The reinterpreta-*

tion of American literature. New York, Harcourt, Brace, 1928. p.139-59.

457. —— *Main currents in American thought.* New York, Harcourt, Brace [c1930] v.3 (*The beginnings of critical realism in America, 1860-1920*), p.329-34 and passim.

458. Pattee, Fred Lewis. *The development of the American short story.* New York, Harper, 1923. p.337-39.

459. —— *A history of American literature since 1870.* New York, Century, 1915. p.398-400.

460. —— *The new American literature, 1890-1930.* New York, London, Century [c1930] p.36-48 and passim.

461. Peixotto, Ernest. "Romanticist under the skin," *Saturday Review of Literature* 9:613-15 May 27, 1933.

462. "The persisting influence of Frank Norris," *Current Literature* 52:227-28 February 1912.

463. Phillips, Marion B. *Aspects of the naturalistic novel in America.* Unpublished M.A. thesis, University of California, 1922. 104p.

464. Piper, Henry Dan. "Frank Norris and Scott Fitzgerald," *Huntington Library Quarterly* 19:393-400 August 1956.

465. Pizer, Donald. "Another look at *The octopus,*" *Nineteenth Century Fiction* 10:217-24 December 1955.

465a. ——"Romantic individualism in Garland, Norris and Crane," *American Quarterly* 10:463-75 Winter 1958.

466. Pollock, Channing. *Harvest of my years, an auto-*

biography. Indianapolis, Bobbs-Merrill [c1943] passim.

467. Preston, Harriet Waters. "The novels of Mr. Norris," *Atlantic Monthly* 91:691-92 May 1903.

468. Quinn, Arthur Hobson. *American fiction.* New York, Appleton-Century [c1936] p.624-30.

469. Rainsford, W. S. "Frank Norris," *World's Work* 5:3276 April 1903.

470. Ramsay, Orrington Cozzens. *Frank Norris and environment.* Unpublished Ph.D. dissertation, University of Wisconsin, 1950. 360p. (Abstract in Wisconsin. University. *Summaries of doctoral dissertations* 11:355-56 1951)

471. Rankin, Thomas Ernest, and Wilford M. Aikin. *American literature.* New York, Harcourt, Brace [c1922] p.257-58.

472. Reninger, H. Willard. "Norris explains *The octopus*: a correlation of his theory and practice," *American Literature* 12:218-27 May 1940.

473. Rosa, Matthew Whiting. *Frank Norris.* Unpublished M.A. thesis, Columbia University, 1929. 78p.

474. Salvan, Albert Jacques. *Zola aux États-Unis.* Providence, Brown University, 1943. p.166-74 and passim. (Brown University Studies. 8) (Ph.D. dissertation, Columbia University, 1942)

475. Scheffauer, Herman George. "Amerikanische Literatur der Gegenwart," *Deutsche Rundschau* 186: 215-22 February 1921.

476. Sherwood, John C. "Norris and the Jeannette," *Philological Quarterly* 37:245-52 April 1958.

477. "A significant novel," *Outlook* 73:152-54 January 17, 1903.

478. Sinclair, Upton Beall. "The California octopus," in his *Mammonart*. Pasadena, Published by the author [c1925] p.349-52.
479. Snell, George. *The shapers of American fiction, 1798-1947*. New York, E. P. Dutton, 1947. p.226-33 and passim.
480. Spiller, Robert Ernest. "Problem in dynamics: Adams, Norris, Robinson," in his *Cycle of American literature*. New York, Macmillan, 1955. p.184-210 and passim.
481. ——, and others. *Literary history of the United States*. New York, Macmillan, 1948. v.2, p.1026; v.3, p.668-69 and passim.
482. Stanton, Theodore. *A manual of American literature*. New York and London, Putnam's, 1909. p.230-31.
483. Stephens, Henry Morse. "The work of Frank Norris: an appreciation," *University of California Chronicle* 5:324-31 January 1903.
484. Strong, Austin. "The 'Frank Norris'," *Saturday Review of Literature* 27:13 July 1, 1944.
485. Swerdlow, Harry. *Naturalism in Frank Norris*. Unpublished M.A. thesis, Cornell University, 1940. 87p.
486. Taylor, Walter Fuller. "Frank Norris," in *The economic novel in America*. Chapel Hill, University of North Carolina Press, 1942. p.282-306.
487. —— *A history of American letters*. Boston, New York, American Book Company [c1936] p.312-15 and passim.
488. Todd, Frank M. "Frank Norris, student, author, and man," *University of California Magazine* 8:349-56 November 1902.

489. Underwood, John Curtis. *Literature and insurgency.* New York, M. Kennerley, 1914. p.130-78.

490. "An unfinished literary career," *Literary Digest* 25:593 November 8, 1902.

491. Valério, A. "Frank Norris, sa vie—son oeuvre." *Revue de l'enseignement des langues vivantes* 32:330-35, 377-96; 33:49-62 September-October 1915; February 1916.

492. Van Doren, Carl and Mark Van Doren. *American and British literature since 1890.* New York, London, D. Appleton-Century [c1939] p.62-64 and passim.

493. Van Doren, Carl. *The American novel, 1789-1939.* Rev.ed. New York, Macmillan, 1940. passim.

494. —— "Frank Norris," in *Columbia University course in literature.* New York, Columbia University Press, 1929. v.18, p.481-83.

495. —— "The later novel," in *Cambridge history of American literature.* New York, Putnam, 1917-23. v.3, p.93-94.

496. Wagenknecht, Edward Charles. "The achievement of Frank Norris," in his *Cavalcade of the American novel.* New York, Holt [1952] p.216-22.

497. —— "Frank Norris in retrospect," *Virginia Quarterly Review* 6:313-20 April 1930.

498. Walcutt, Charles Child. *American literary naturalism, a divided stream.* Minneapolis, University of Minnesota Press [c1956] p.114-56 and passim.

499. —— "Frank Norris and the search for form," *University of Kansas City Review* 14:126-36 Winter 1947.

500. —— "Frank Norris on realism and naturalism," *American Literature* 13:61-63 March 1941.

501. ——"The naturalism of *Vandover and the brute*," in O'Connor, William Van, ed. *Forms of modern fiction; essays collected in honor of Joseph Warren Beach.* Minneapolis, University of Minnesota Press [1948] p.254-68.

502. Wales, Anita Marie. *The development of Frank Norris as a writer of fiction.* Unpublished M.A. thesis, University of California, 1918. 41p.

503. Walker, Franklin Dickerson. *Frank Norris; a biographical and critical study.* Unpublished Ph.D. dissertation, University of California (Berkeley), 1932. 361p. (Abstract in California. University. Graduate Division. *Programmes of final public examinations,* 1932)

504. ——*Frank Norris, a biography.* Garden City, Doubleday, Doran, 1932. 317p.

505. ——"Frank Norris at the University of California," *University of California Chronicle* 33:320-49 July 1931. (Includes a "List of writings by Frank Norris, published during his attendance at the University of California, 1890-1894")

506. Werner, William Louser. *Frank Norris.* Unpublished M.A. thesis, Pennsylvania State University, 1922. 56p.

507. Williams, Harold Herbert. *Modern English writers.* London, Sidgwick, 1925. p.491-92.

508. Williams, Talcott. "Fiction read and written in 1901," *Review of Reviews* 24:591 November 1901.

509. Wilson, Edmund. *Classics and commercials.* New York, Farrar, Straus [1950] p.50.

510. Wister, Owen. "*The pit*—a story of Chicago: the last and best novel of the late Frank Norris," *World's Work* 5:3133-34 February 1903.

511. Wood, William Allen. "A golden bowl broken," *Phi Gamma Delta* 25:157-63 December 1902.

512. Wright, H. M. "In memoriam — Frank Norris, 1870-1902," *University of California Chronicle* 5:240-45 October 1902.

513. Wyatt, Edith. "Vandover and the brute," in her *Great companions.* New York, D. Appleton, 1917. p.48-58.

Reviews

514. *Yvernelle* (1892)
    Critic 19:316 December 5, 1891.
    New York Herald December 13, 1891, p.26b.
    Overland Monthly 19:106 January 1892.
    Publishers' Weekly Christmas Bookshelf 40,nos.21-22:36 November 21-28 1891.
515. *Moran of the Lady Letty* (1898)
    Literary World 29:404 November 26, 1898.
    Literature 3:577-79 December 17, 1898. (William Dean Howells)
    Louisville Times November 26, 1898, p.7, col.4. (Isaac Marcosson)
    Public Opinion 25:473 October 13, 1898.
516. *McTeague* (1899)
    Academy 57:746 December 23, 1899.
    American Review of Reviews 19:749 June 1899.
    Athenaeum 2,no.3762:757 December 2, 1899.
    Book Buyer 18:244 April 1899. (E. D. Beach)
    Bookman (London) 17:121 January 1900.
    Bookman (New York) 9:356-57 June 1899. (Nancy Huston Banks)
    Critic 34:398 May 1899. (Jeannette Gilder)
    Independent 51:968 April 6, 1899.
    Literary News 20:109 April 1899.
    Literary World 30:99 April 1, 1899.
    Literature n.s.1:241-42 March 24, 1899. (William Dean Howells)
    Louisville Times March 13, 1899, p.6, col.5. (Isaac Marcosson)
    New York Tribune March 5, 1899, p.14b.
    Outlook 61:646-47 March 18, 1899.

517\. *Blix* (1899)
Academy 59:111-12 August 11, 1900.
Argonaut 45:9 October 16, 1899.
Land of Sunshine 11:353 November 1899. (Charles F. Lummis)
Louisville Times November 13, 1899, p.6, col.5. (Isaac Marcosson)
Overland Monthly 34:474-75 November 1899.

518\. *A man's woman* (1900)
Athenaeum 2,no.3809:547 October 27, 1900.
Critic 36:352-53 April 1900.
Land of Sunshine 12:385 May 1900. (Charles F. Lummis)
Literary World 31:140 July 1, 1900.
Outlook 64:486 March 3, 1900.
Public Opinion 28:281-82 March 1, 1900.

519\. *The octopus* (1901)
Arena 27:547-54 May 1902. (B. O. Flower)
Athenaeum 2,no.3858:447-48 October 5, 1901.
Atlantic Monthly 89:708-09 May 1902. (H. W. Boynton)
Book Buyer 22:326-28 May 1901. (A. S. Van Westrum)
Bookman (New York) 13:245-47 May 1901. (F. T. Cooper)
Dial 31:136 September 1, 1901. (William M. Payne)
Harper's Monthly 103:824 October 1901.
Independent 53:1139-40 May 16, 1901.
Land of Sunshine 15:58 July 1901. (Charles F. Lummis)
Louisville Times April 13, 1901, p.13, col.6. (Isaac Marcosson)
Overland Monthly 37:1050-51 May 1901.

Town Talk (San Francisco) 9,no.451:24-26 April 20, 1901.

520. *The pit* (1903)

Academy 64:153-54 February 14, 1903.
Arena 29:440-42 April 1903. (B. O. Flower)
Athenaeum 2,no.3929:204-05 February 14, 1903.
Book News Monthly 21:437-38 February 1903.
Bookman (London) 23:246-47 March 1903.
Bookman (New York) 16:565-67 February 1903. (Albert B. Paine)
Dial 34:242 April 1, 1903. (William Morton Payne)
Harper's Weekly 47:433 March 14, 1903.
Independent 55:331-32 February 5, 1903.
Lamp 26:54-56 February 1903. (A. S. Van Westrum)
Literary Digest 26:353 March 7, 1903.
Literary World 34:54 March 1903.
New York Evening Sun January 24, 1903, p.5.
Outlook 73:152-54 January 17, 1903.
World's Work 5:3133-34 February 1903. (Owen Wister)

521. *The responsibilities of the novelist* (1903)

Critic 43:576 December 1903.
Lamp 27:342-44 November 1903.
Nation 77:411-12 November 19, 1903.
Out West 19:688 December 1903.
Outlook 75:829-30 December 1903.
Public Opinion 35:536 October 22, 1903.

522. *A deal in wheat* (1903)

Academy 65:500,502 November 7, 1903.
Athenaeum 2,no.3967:613 November 7, 1903.
Book News Monthly 22:123 October 1903.

Bookman (New York) 18:311-12 November 1903. (F. T. Cooper)
Literary News 24:322-23 November 1903.
Reader 2:635-36 November 1903.

523. *The third circle* (1909)
Academy 77:419 August 14, 1909.
Athenaeum 2,no.4269:206 August 21, 1909.
Nation 88:607 June 17, 1909.
New York Times Book Review 14:339 May 29, 1909; 14:377 June 12, 1909.
Saturday Review 108:264 August 28, 1909.
Spectator 103:425 September 18, 1909.

524. *Vandover and the brute* (1914)
American Review of Reviews 49:761 June 1914.
Athenaeum no.4522:886 June 27, 1914.
Atlantic Monthly 114:525 October 1914.
Bookman (London) 46:216-17 August 1914. (Harold Vallings)
Bookman (New York) 39:444-45 June 1914. (F. T. Cooper)
Independent 79:173 August 3, 1914.
Literary Digest 48:1494-95 June 20, 1914.
Nation 98:432-33 April 16, 1914.
New York Times Book Review 19:181 April 12, 1914.
Outlook 107:264 May 30, 1914.
Saturday Review 117:805 June 20, 1914.

525. *Frank Norris of "The Wave"* (1931)
American Literature 3:349-50 November 1931. (C. H. Grattan)
New York Herald Tribune Books August 23, 1931, p.13. (F. H. Britten)
New York Times Book Review May 3, 1931, p.2. (John Chamberlain)

INDEX

INDEX

(Numbers refer to items)

ERRATUM

Item 24, line 22, on page 33, 'Introuction' should read Introduction.

Item 49, line 4, on page 40, 'TALOR' should read TAYLOR.

Item 50, line 18, page 41, 'Perveted' should read Perverted.

DESIGNED AND PRINTED BY ROBERT GREENWOOD
AND NEWTON BAIRD AT THE TALISMAN PRESS
SEPTEMBER ⊤ 1959